IMAGES
of America

THE JAMBOREE IN WHEELING

On the Cover: A partial early-1960s cast picture forms the cover of this *Jamboree* book. The full picture appears on two pages in chapter three. (Williams family collection.)

IMAGES of America
THE JAMBOREE IN WHEELING

Ivan M. Tribe and Jacob L. Bapst
Foreword by Barbara "Peeper Williams" Smik

Copyright © 2020 by Ivan M. Tribe and Jacob L. Bapst
ISBN 978-1-4671-0568-2

Published by Arcadia Publishing
Charleston, South Carolina

Printed in the United States of America

Library of Congress Control Number: 2020937896

For all general information, please contact Arcadia Publishing:
Telephone 843-853-2070
Fax 843-853-0044
E-mail sales@arcadiapublishing.com
For customer service and orders:
Toll-Free 1-888-313-2665

Visit us on the Internet at www.arcadiapublishing.com

Barbara "Peeper" Smik, aided by sisters Madeline and Karen, have kept the Jamboree memories alive.

Contents

Foreword		6
Acknowledgments		7
Introduction		8
1.	The Early Years: 1933–1945	11
2.	The Golden Years: 1946–1962	39
3.	Decline and Rejuvenation: 1962–1970	77
4.	Changing Focus: 1971–1983	89
5.	Jamboree Bluegrass: 1948–2020	101
6.	Fading in the Sunset—Almost: 1983–2020	111

FOREWORD

The *Jamboree* in Wheeling has always had a good friend in Ivan Tribe. He has written many books and articles about the pioneers in country and bluegrass music and has extensive knowledge of their history. Professor Tribe and his wife, Deanna, enjoy playing the old-time music on their Sunday broadcasts over WOUB-FM in Athens, Ohio.

My two sisters and I were discussing recently what "growing up country" meant to each of us. To us, it is the lifelong friendships we gained through the *Jamboree*. There are the entertainers we so very much admire, the disc jockeys who played the records, the historians who researched and wrote the articles and the books, and the fans who became like family over the years. I often heard other entertainers say that "if you have a fan of your music, they will be fans for life."

Over their long careers, my mom and dad received many loving letters from *Jamboree* fans. Here are few excerpts: from Ontario, Canada, "Live radio was wonderful. You were like really nice folks who dropped by (via the radio) for a visit."; from Maine, "Thank you for the songs about coping with our losses, making the best from what we have, and with faith and hope we carry on."; and from Labrador, Canada, "Growing up in the 1960s was a hard and harsh time in a small community, but your songs often kept us going."

Back in the 1970s, I remember reading a book of reflections by the great cellist Pablo Casals. He said that music must serve a purpose and be a part of something larger than itself and that music is something to be approached with integrity.

That is what music and the *Jamboree* meant to me. It was entertainers singing their songs over live radio and bringing encouragement and happiness to their listeners. It was music serving a purpose.

Thank you, Ivan Tribe and Jacob Bapst, for writing this book and asking me to write the foreword. What an honor!

—Barbara "Peeper Williams" Smik,
Oldest daughter of country music pioneers Doc and Chickie Williams

Acknowledgments

In 1979, the senior half of this team was asked if he could write a history of country music in West Virginia, a task which focused on the role of live radio programming. The Mountain State had several significant radio stations, but none as much as WWVA Wheeling with its powerful nighttime broadcast. This signal reached into all or part of 18 states and 6 Canadian provinces, mostly north and east of Wheeling. The station's Saturday night *Jamboree* program attracted fans and listeners in those areas that could not pull in shows from Nashville, Chicago, and more distant locales; thus, the *Jamboree* ranked as one of the nation's top outlets for country music. Having first been to the show in 1966 and intermittently thereafter and gathered numerous photographs, records, and songbooks, it seemed we had a pretty good start amassing material for this volume, an assumption that proved shortsighted.

A number of friends and fans of the *Jamboree* came forward to fill in the gap. Back in the early days of *Mountaineer Jamboree: Country Music in West Virginia* (1984) research, a key figure had been the legendary Doc and Chickie Williams. Friendships also developed with Wilma Lee Cooper, Lee Moore, and Patti Powell. This time, Doc and Chickie's daughter Barbara Smik took the lead aided by her sisters Madeline and Karen. Other key sources of photographs included Jo Anne Davis, Dave Sichak, David Heath of WWOV-FM, Terrence McGill, John Morris, and Richard Weize of Bear Family Records. All of these and a few others are credited for their contributions to each caption. Those images unaccredited are from the author's collection. Others supplied advice, direction, information, and council: the late Virginia Alderman, Fred Bartenstein, Buddy Griffin, George Hausser, Bob and Lee Ann Turbanic, and our own wives, Josie Bapst and Deanna Tribe. To all of these and anyone accidentally overlooked, we are grateful. Also, we regret that we could not include every *Jamboree* performer; there were just too many!

INTRODUCTION

Beginning in the mid-1920s, radio stations that directed their appeal to rural folk and recent urban migrants sponsored broadcasts on Saturday—and sometimes Friday—live audience programs generically termed "barn dances." The first of these, *The National Barn Dance* from WLS Chicago, began in 1924. The next year, WSM Nashville inaugurated what soon became the still running *Grand Ole Opry*. These two presentations were followed by others, including *The Big D Jamboree* from KRLD Dallas, the *Louisiana Hayride* from KWKH Shreveport, the *Tennessee Barn Dance* from WNOX Knoxville, the *Midwestern Hayride* from WLW Cincinnati, and the *Jamboree* from WWVA Wheeling, West Virginia. Down-home music and bucolic comedy comprised the content of such fare. By the 1980s, all of these shows had fallen victim to changing times except for the *Opry* and the *Jamboree* in Wheeling, which continued through December 2005.

WWVA radio took to the airwaves in December 1926 with 50 watts of power and, by July 1929, had increased its strength to 5,000 watts. In March 1932, the station became a property of the Storer Broadcasting Company. The *Jamboree* from WWVA originated as a studio presentation on January 7, 1933, and opened to live audiences from April 1 as the brainchild of George W. Smith, who became managing director in 1931. Smith possessed a fertile mind that viewed radio in a manner similar to what Henry Ford saw in autos, that it could become something of a societal equalizer or "level all humanity." His writing contains such phrases as "it has been our privilege [WWVA] to enter the humble mountaineer cabin." Or, as longtime musical artist Doc Williams said, he saw its "potential." What's more, as WWVA historian Virginia Alderman pointed out, "The Saturday night *Jamboree* with its homespun style . . . was a welcome diversion to the thousands of depression weary listeners." Assuming that the *Jamboree* was a major part of Smith's objective, it may have done little at leveling society, but as a radio institution, it thrived for 72 years on WWVA and still survives in a modest scale on a small independent FM station.

Initially known as the *Midnight Jamboree*, the live show opened on April 17, 1933, before an audience of over 3,000 people at downtown Wheeling's spacious Capitol Theater. Through ensuing years, the *Jamboree* was held in various downtown venues but eventually settled into the Wheeling Market Auditorium. By the end of the decade, the name had become the *World's Original Jamboree*. In the beginning, talent tended to consist of local amateur and semiprofessional musicians. The cast became increasingly professional as the years advanced. Station management added daily programming where musicians presented shows in quarter-hour and half-hour segments and played live shows in the station's eastern Ohio, northern West Virginia, and western Pennsylvania listening area that supplemented their incomes. Schoolhouses, veterans' halls, and other public places served as locales for these presentations, often held as fundraisers for PTAs, granges, volunteer fire departments, and other local clubs. These early morning and midday shows shared prominence through the mid-1950s when they were phased out. Artists, however, continued doing personal appearances on the basis of their *Jamboree* affiliation.

During its first decade, the *Jamboree* endured not only the Great Depression, which gripped the upper Ohio Valley, but periodic floods (especially 1936) and eventually World War II. From 1939 through 1942, most of the cast went on weeklong tours of regional cities bringing entertainment to the area but always returned to Wheeling on Saturday night. An audience boost of major proportion took place on October 8, 1942, when WWVA became a 50,000-watt station with a nighttime signal that blanketed much of the northeastern United States and several Canadian provinces. With gasoline rationing, the live audience portion of the *Jamboree* was discontinued from December 1942 until the end of the international conflict. As many male entertainers entered military service, the studio version of the *Jamboree* continued with increased female personnel doing their part to maintain morale on the home front.

With the cession of hostilities, director Smith made plans to rejuvenate the live *Jamboree* bigger and better than ever, which indeed happened although Smith himself passed away on May 9, some weeks prior to the relaunch at the Virginia Theater on July 13, 1946. There it began 16 years of continuous Saturday night broadcasting. All radio programs encounter highs and lows during a long run, but the Virginia Theater era certainly ranked as the zenith for the *Jamboree*. With a generally prosperous economy, the venerable program usually played to capacity crowds. Although network radio was in decline for several years in the mid-1950s, the *Jamboree* had a national CBS affiliation, which, by all accounts, made their artists more marketable with the country music fan base. This also constituted the period when the best-known *Jamboree* stars were hitting their so-called prime, chief among them Big Slim, the Lone Cowboy (Harry C. McAuliffe); Wilma Lee and Stoney Cooper; Hawkshaw Hawkins; Lee and Juanita Moore; the Osborne Brothers; and Doc and Chickie Williams.

The demise of the Virginia Theater in July 1962 led to a low point as the new *Jamboree* home, the Rex Theater, was too small to accommodate large crowds—about 900 people capacity. Still, it continued with diminishing gate receipts until veteran vocalist Mac Wiseman took over management and secured a new base—the Wheeling Island Exhibition Hall—from January 15, 1966, to December 6, 1969. It could comfortably accommodate 2,500–3,000 fans on folding chairs. He introduced a monthly guest star system whereby a "big name" from Nashville would appear on the program for a reduced fee, but in exchange, the star's recordings would receive hourly airplay seven days a week for the month prior to the guest appearance. This led to a bigger gate at the *Jamboree* that night and more airplay, which, on a 50,000-watt station, could almost alone make at least a moderate hit and produce enough monetary surplus to cover times when the attendance would be fewer.

On December 13, 1969, the *Jamboree* relocated back to downtown Wheeling and the Capitol Theater from whence it first appeared as a live audience show. It remained there until December 2005. The Capitol was bought by WWVA, renamed the Capitol Music Hall, and the station placed its studios in the building. The station management nationalized the program, renaming it *Jamboree USA*. The Capitol was similar to the "movie palaces" that had once dominated downtowns of major cities and could accommodate over 3,000 fans. It might fill twice in a night if the guest was a country superstar with the stature of a Johnny Cash or a Buck Owens.

By the late 1970s, the monthly guest plan had increased to three or four times a month. While this kept the show popular and continued to attract an audience, it led to a diminishing status for the regular *Jamboree* performers who found themselves relegated to becoming "warm-up acts" for the weekly guest stars. Even then, they might actually appear on the program only six or eight times yearly. Still being a *Jamboree USA* member carried some weight even if less than in 1954. The artists who did best under these conditions were those who were long-established, such as Doc and Chickie Williams or the newer team of Bob Gallion and Patti Powell, who, if not major stars, were in sufficient demand to earn a decent living by combining their artistry with the operation of a booking agency. Others like Johnny Russell stayed long enough to have a hit record, which allowed him to become established in Nashville and eventually attain *Grand Ole Opry* membership while 1966–1970 manager Mac Wiseman did the same. Although never an *Opry* member, Wiseman did achieve elevation to both the Bluegrass and Country Music Halls of Fame. Other *Jamboree* artists from the latter years either found work in the clubs in cities like Pittsburgh or satisfied themselves with part-time work as entertainers. In the intervening years, ownership of WWVA radio moved from Storer Broadcasting in 1962 to Basic Communications, Inc., and a decade later to Screen Gems Radio Inc., a division of Columbia Pictures.

In 1977, with music festivals (rock, blues, bluegrass, and more) becoming widespread nationally, F. Glenn Reeves, who then served as *Jamboree USA*'s executive director, persuaded his corporate managers that a giant country music festival could be a success. Thus was born *Jamboree in the Hills* near St. Clairsville, Ohio, in mid-July, which became an instant success, attracting a crowd estimated at 20,000 that first summer. Crowd sizes increased to over 30,000 in later years, dwarfing the sizes of attendees at the Capitol Theater. The biggest country stars—typified by Johnny Cash, Charlie Pride, and Crystal Gayle—served as major attractions from the very beginning. Even though an annual three-day event, the very success of *Jamboree in the Hills* seemed to further diminish the stature of Saturday night shows back at the theater on Wheeling's Main Street and on AM radio.

Nonetheless, *Jamboree USA* continued forward, celebrating a golden anniversary in 1983 with appropriate ceremony. In addition to recently prominent guests such as Billy "Crash" Craddock and Charlie Pride, popular figures from the 1950s typified by Betty Cody and Dusty Owens were inducted along with a total figure of 50 persons who had helped make the program significant. The venerable *Jamboree* went forward into its sixth decade, maintaining the format that had dominated for the past several years.

Few institutions endure forever in this field or otherwise. The annual *Jamboree in the Hills*, while a *Jamboree* outreach in a manner of speaking and hugely successful, diminished the stature of the indoor radio program. An August 1992 article in the authoritative magazine, the *Journal of the American Academy for the Preservation of Old Time Country Music*, celebrated the show's survival while somewhat decrying the declining influence of regular performers ranging from old-timers like Doc Williams who were with WWVA longer than Roy Acuff with WSM, to more recent figures typified by Leon Douglas, Darnell Miller, and Junior Norman.

As the *Jamboree* moved into the new century, the venerable presentation, which was outside the perimeter of current thinking among newer radio management, may have been living on borrowed time. Finally, at the end of 2005, *Jamboree USA* terminated. *Jamboree in the Hills* continued through 2018 but was canceled in 2019, and as of that December, its future remained in doubt. Some local fans in the area hoped for revival, while others believed that the program was dead. Efforts for a newly incorporated *Wheeling Jamboree* had mixed but generally disappointing results. Radio broadcasts tended to be on small FM stations, such as WWOV. Some of the signals barely reached beyond the Wheeling city limits and could hardly attract an audience to sustain the program. Live audiences generally numbered a few hundred or less. Artists such as Shana Smith, Darnell Miller, or Larry Efaw's Bluegrass Pioneers displayed real talent, but small numbers of fans could not supply much support.

In the final analysis, the *Jamboree* deserves to be celebrated for what it did contribute to a successful American art form. Only the *Grand Ole Opry* has outlasted the program, and one might argue that even its quality and stature is not what it had been. Like the blues, born in the poor sections of African American communities, country music came to life in rural America in communities dominated by lower- and lower-middle-class Caucasians who eventually entered the American mainstream. For this alone, the program deserves fond remembrance.

One

THE EARLY YEARS
1933–1945

The *Jamboree* originated as a show by George Smith to showcase local practitioners of downhome music from the available pool of area amateurs and semiprofessionals found in Wheeling and neighboring towns. Young Bill Jones from Martin's Ferry, Ohio, was one while Elmer Crowe and Fred Craddock & his Happy Five came from Moundsville. Near to Wheeling, the Tweedy Brothers were professionals having made phonograph records and playing county fairs since 1924. The comical Italians Tony and Dominic supplied humor, and station announcer Howard Donahoe provided balance and kept the program on track.

Crowe remained until 1940, and Jones alternated between New York and Wheeling into the mid-1940s, but professional musicians soon eclipsed the locals. By having weekday shows, they managed to make a modest living in the depression-wracked economy. Chief among them was "Cowboy" Loye (Pack) first on radio in Nebraska; the trio of Cap, Andy and Flip, veterans of the network-based *Lum & Abner* Show; Jake Taylor and His Railsplitters; and most professional of all, Hugh (Cross) and Shug's (Fisher) Radio Pals, who were sometimes known as "the Georgie Porgie Boys" when sponsored by the breakfast food. After three or four years, they all went on to work elsewhere. Others took their place, including Marshall "Grandpa" Jones, who worked two different times at WWVA, whereas Doc Williams and the Border Riders, who came in 1937 from Pittsburgh, spent virtually their whole career there, as did Big Slim, the Lone Cowboy, who soon followed him.

Other newcomers in the later 1930s included Frankie More and His Log Cabin Girls (or Gang, depending on personnel); Joe Barker and wife, Little Shirley; future Hall of Fame member Floyd Tillman; and medicine show veteran Lew Childre. From 1930 through 1942, station management took a whole group of *Jamboree* entertainers on weeklong Goodwill Tours to regional cities such as Steubenville and Youngstown, Ohio, and Greensburg, Pennsylvania, leaving some back at WWVA to keep the daily shows going. The station went to 50,000 watts in October 1942, but with the nation plunged into World War II, gasoline rationing, defense plants, and military duty meant discontinuing the live show until mid-1946. The remaining men, along with more women, manned the microphones. Thus, while the *Jamboree* had a much-increased audience on the airwaves, it had virtually no live viewers until peace returned.

Silver Yodelin' Bill Jones (1909–?) had one of the longest associations with WWVA of anyone, actually singing on the station as early as 1927, six years before the *Jamboree* started. In between stints in Wheeling, he also spent several years in New York working radio with Denver Darling and band. A longtime resident of nearby Bridgeport, Ohio, he often appeared at reunion shows. He is pictured (seated) with his unidentified band members, the Panhandle Rangers.

Silver Yodelin' Bill Jones, in as fine a voice as ever, appeared at a country music old-time radio concert in Charleston in May 1979. Other *Jamboree* old-timers who also played included Doc and Chickie Williams, Lee Moore, and Donna Darlene as well as old-timers from Charleston, Fairmont, Beckley, and Bluefield. The program provided younger country fans with a sampling of the "Golden Age" of how old-time hillbilly radio might have sounded.

Elmer Crow (1909–1978) was a *Jamboree* mainstay in the early years, singing old songs and also showing some flair for comedy as pictured in the photograph below using his guitar strings in a bow and arrow–type skit with Fred Gardini (accordion) and other station personnel. A proud member of both the Elks and Knights of Pythias, as illustrated by his lapel button, he lived in the area and sometimes attended *Jamboree* reunions into the early 1970s. Sadly, he made no recordings.

The trio of Warren Caplinger (1889–1957), Andy Patterson (1893–1950), and Flip Strickland (1908–1990), known as Cap, Andy & Flip (pictured here from left to right), organized in Akron in 1932 and successively worked at WWVA, WMMN, and WCHS. As time passed, Flip left in 1940, replaced by Milt Patterson, and the trio continued until 1949. They eventually concentrated on sacred music. (Williams family collection.)

Shorty Fincher (1899–1958) and his Cotton Pickers was a country band who played at the *Jamboree* in 1939. Personnel included, from left to right, Hamilton "Rawhide" Fincher, Shorty Fincher, Lonesome Valley Sally (Alexandra Kaspura), Tommy Nott, and Dolph Hewitt. While the Finchers were Alabama natives, the others were Pennsylvanians. With slightly different members, they recorded for OKeh in 1934 as the Crazy Hillbillies.

Dolph Hewitt (1914–1996), a West Finley, Pennsylvania, native worked at the *Jamboree* playing both fiddle and guitar and singing with such acts as those of Shorty Fincher and Frankie More. After World War II, he joined the *National Barn Dance* in Chicago, working with the Sage Riders and as a solo vocalist. Recording for RCA Victor, he became known as "King of the Barn Dance."

Calvin "Curley" Miller (1914–1994) had a long association with the *Jamboree*, scattered over several different years: 1938–1942, 1945–1948, and several years from 1959. His sister Millie Wayne was also a *Jamboree* favorite. Sometimes, Curley worked in tandem with Joe Barker's group and sometime with his own Plowboy group. He also worked at WLS Chicago and KDKA Pittsburgh and worked as a horse trainer and radio announcer.

Hugh Ballard Cross (1903–1970) had a varied musical career that took him from his Tennessee birthplace to such locales as Atlanta, Knoxville, Chicago, and Cincinnati as well as three stints in Wheeling (1933–1937, 1939, and late 1940s). On Columbia Records in the late 1920s, he did duets with the legendary Riley Puckett and an early recording of "Wabash Cannonball." At WWVA, he and Shug Fisher led the Radio Pals, which included Fred Giardini, and recorded 14 sides for Decca in 1937. Later, he worked solo. (Williams family collection.)

Oklahoma native George "Shug" Fisher (1907–1984) had one of the most varied careers in American music being not only a member of the Radio Pals at WWVA, but also the Sons of the Pioneers, and he recorded on Capitol Records and cut numerous transcriptions. In the 1950s, he was a member of the *Ozark Jubilee* on ABC television. In addition, he played numerous roles as a character actor on such programs as *Gunsmoke*, *Ripcord*, and *The Beverly Hillbillies*.

Hugh Cross (1903–1970) and Shug Fisher (1907–1984), with their Radio Pals, worked at the *Jamboree* for up to four years until late 1937. They were sometimes called "the Georgie Porgie Boys" for a cereal sponsor. A young Doc Williams thought them the epitome of professionalism. Cross is at far right, with Fisher to his left. The others likely included Ted Grant (1905–1969) and Fred Gardini (d. 1988).

Hugh Cross and Shug Fisher's Radio Pals included a variety of members in the group at different times. This lineup consisted of a total of four, with the additional two being the versatile Lennie Aleshire, a Missourian noted for playing unusual instruments, and Lonnie Glosson, best known for his harmonica skills. Aleshire also worked with Grandpa Jones and, later, as half of Lennie and Goo Goo at the *Ozark Jubilee*.

After leaving Bradley Kincaid, Grandpa Jones (1913–1998) came to WWVA in 1937 as a solo performer but did personal appearances with the Rhythm Rangers, consisting of, from left to right, Pete Rentschler, Floyd Houser, and Loren Bledsoe. The woman beside him in the first row is Mary Ann Estes (1919–2005), later better known as the wife of well-known West Virginia musician Buddy Starcher.

Loye "Cowboy Loye" Pack (1900–1941) came to WWVA as a solo performer in 1933 but soon added "Just Plain" John Oldham to his act. Well remembered both as an entertainer and on-air salesman, by the time he moved to WMMN Fairmont early in 1937, his Bluebonnet Troupe, named for sponsor Bluebonnet Crystals, totaled nine musicians.

Cowboy Loye led one of the most successful *Jamboree* touring groups in the mid-1930s, taking its name from sponsor Bluebonnet Crystals. Standing from left to right are Custer Allen (?), Cowboy Loye, unidentified, Ray Myers, Just Plain John Oldham (?), James "Sheepherder" Moore, Jake Taylor, and French "Curly" Mitchell.

James Moore (1869–1950), known on stage as "Sheepherder," worked as a fiddler with the much more fondly remembered Cowboy Loye at WWVA. Later, he moved with Loye to WMMN Fairmont and also worked with Jake Taylor and the Rail Splitters after World War II until old age caught up with him. Allegedly a native of Nebraska (where he must have met Loye), Moore was remembered as living a very frugal lifestyle.

The elderly fiddler James "Sheepherder" Moore had a humorous side, as he revealed in this publicity stunt on downtown Wheeling's Main Street wearing a signboard about the *Jamboree* fiddling contest. At various times, Moore worked with both Cowboy Loye and Jake Taylor.

Jack Dunigan (1909–1993) and Gertrude Miller (1915–1967) were a husband-wife team who worked at WWVA and numerous other stations from the late 1930s well into the 1950s. Dunigan had been a member of Clayton McMichen's Georgia Wildcats. With their Trail Blazers, they are, from left to right, (seated) Miller; (standing) Fiddlin' Red Herron, Chief Red Hawk, Tommy Sutton, Bud DeCarlo, Dunigan. In later years, Dunigan became a deejay at WJTN Jamestown, New York.

Mary Calvas (1919–1959), known as "Sunflower," was from Davis, West Virginia. She worked for many years as a vocalist-bass player with Doc Williams's Border Riders, during which time she married Doc's fiddling brother Cy Williams (Milo Smik). The marriage collapsed during World War II, and Sunflower teamed with Froggie Cortez, playing at WKST New Castle, Pennsylvania. She later married Eddie Wallace of the Sunshine Boys but passed away from cancer at the age of 40. Her nickname came from her sunny disposition.

James "Froggie" Cortez (1914–?) played comedy with Doc Williams's Border Riders from 1937 until Doc disbanded his group during the war. He sang humorous songs like "Courtin' in the Rain" and had a trained monkey is his act. In later years, he worked at New Castle, Pennsylvania, with Mary "Sunflower" Calvas and then Jake Taylor.

Alabama-born Hamilton "Rawhide" Fincher (1911–c. 1980s) was an early-day comedian who worked with both his brother Shorty's band and Doc Williams. Back with Shorty in 1946, he had altered his name to "Cowhide." Pictured here with his family, he later lived in Pennsylvania.

Jake Taylor (1914–1974) came to WWVA in 1934 and remained until 1937, when he went to WMMN Fairmont. This version of the band shows, from left to right, unidentified, Betty Taylor, Jake Taylor, Jewel "Shorty" Sharpe, and Silver Yodelin' Bill Jones. Taylor composed a song that became a bluegrass standard, "There Ain't Nobody Gonna Miss Me When I'm Gone," but his own recordings were limited to six sides on Cozy and Mercury.

JAKE TAYLOR'S RAIL SPLITTERS

The WWVA listening area's populace included a large portion of east and south European people. Thus, some of the *Jamboree* acts appealed to this particular listening audience. The team of Tony Biccio (or Sciffio) and Dominic Lipari pictured here reflected the region's Italian influences (Steubenville's Dean Martin was part of this community). Later, fans treasured their comic skits.

Frankie More (1906–?), although a musician of sorts, was more of a leader and promoter. He had recorded as one of the Log Cabin Boys in 1934 and came with a group of musicians to WWVA in 1936. Of those pictured here in 1938, "Little Shoe," Dolph "Cob" Hewitt, and Roy "Shorty" Hobbs all made names for themselves later, but the identity of the girl "Jonny" is otherwise unknown.

Alma Crosby (1910–?), who performed under the pseudonym "Little Shoe," came to Wheeling in 1936 as part of Frankie More's Log Cabin Gang and remained there for about five or six years. Her musical banjo style resembled her aunt's, the more-renowned "Cousin Emmy," and songbooks described her as a "small person with a small but pleasing voice." After leaving WWVA, she went to various locales and was at KLRA Little Rock, Arkansas.

Cynthia May Carver (1903–1980), known as "Cousin Emmy," played over a wide variety of radio stations, including WWVA in the late 1930s. A "banjo pickin' gal" from Kentucky, she is best known for originating the later Osborne Brothers classic "Ruby" for Decca Records in 1947. Grandpa Jones credited her with teaching him to play banjo during her stay in Wheeling. She eventually ended her career in California. (Richard Weize and More Bears Archive.)

In her varied later career, Cousin Emmy could pop up in unexpected places. At right is a movie still from *The Second Greatest Sex* (1956) with leading man George Nader. Her role drew little attention, which went to glamour queens Jeanne Crain and blonde bombshell Mamie Van Doren. (Richard Weize and More Bears Archive.)

Blaine Smith (1915–1997), sometimes accompanied by his brother Cal (1912–?), had a musical career that included two stints at WWVA, roughly 1933–1935 and 1946–1947. His style was in some ways more akin to early pop singers like Henry Burr and Vernon Dalhart than to hard country. He benefitted from a repertoire of old songs and good looks, which appealed to younger fans, as well as devotion to his mother (he even sold her pictures over the air). Over the years, he recorded for Vocalion and smaller labels like Dome and Bluebonnet and did radio work in Pittsburgh, Chicago, Fairmont, and New Castle, Pennsylvania. He spent his later musical career on both radio and television in Harrisonburg, Virginia, eventually going into business.

One of the reasons for Blaine Smith's popularity with older radio listeners came not only from his nostalgic songs of the old days, but also because of his reverent attitude toward his mother. He even sold pictures of her over the airwaves and not only on his programs at WWVA, but also during his sojourns in Fairmont, New Castle, and Pittsburgh.

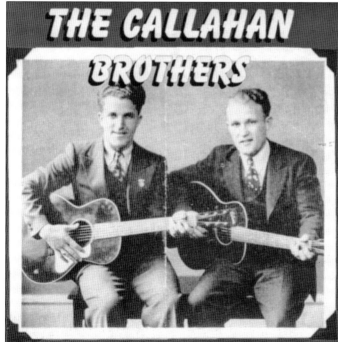

Homer (1912–2002) and Walter (1910–1971), the Callahan Brothers—perhaps better known as Bill and Joe—spent only a few months at the *Jamboree* in 1936 but had a more extensive career in Dallas, Texas. They made numerous recordings for Columbia and fewer for Decca between 1934 and 1951. They appeared in the western movie *Springtime in Texas* in 1945.

Charlie Monroe (1903–1975) carved out a niche of his own in musical annals apart from better-known brother Bill. Prior to his 1939 four-month stint at WWVA, he had only one or two band members, but at the *Jamboree*, he expanded to five. From left to right are (seated) Curly Seckler, Dale Cole, and Tommy Edwards; (standing) Charlie Monroe and Tommy Scott. (Richard Weize and More Bears Archive.)

Another early *Jamboree* musician, Tommy Radcliffe, also appeared in the first cast picture in 1933. Like the others—except for the Tweedy Brothers—he never made recordings (apparently frowned upon by early day WWVA management). At other times, Radcliffe also displayed his musical skills at WCHS Charleston and WMMN Fairmont.

Floyd Houser (front right) had a popular string band at the *Jamboree* in the early years. A key figure was his vocalist-wife Sammi Ashe (front left), known as "Little Sammi." In the 1970s, the Housers attended WWVA reunions.

Harry C. McAuliffe (1903–1966), known as "Big Slim, the Lone Cowboy," played on the *Jamboree* off and on from 1937 until shortly before his death. He first came to WWVA with the Border Riders in 1937 but soon went solo. Recording for Decca in 1936 as "Big Slim Aliff," he later cut discs for small firms in the United States and three albums on the Canadian Arc label. (John Morris collection.)

Not many photographs exist of Big Slim with a full band other than this one from 1942. Personnel included Ray "Quarantine" Brown on comedy and bass, Toby Stroud on fiddle, and Johnny Hill on guitar. Stroud later had his own group on WWVA, and Hill is reported to have been the actual composer of Slim's original classic composition "Sunny Side of the Mountain." (John Morris collection.)

Ray Myers (1911–1986), dubbed the "World Famous Armless Musician," first earned national attention at the 1933 world's fair, after which he went to work with Cowboy Loye at the *Jamboree* several different times. In addition to playing the guitar with his toes and singing, Myers could handle all sorts of things, including driving a car and carpenter work. He is pictured playing with one of his children.

Cricket (left) and Laughing Lindy (right) worked as a girl duet with the larger unit of Frankie More's Log Cabin Girls in the late 1930s and early 1940s. Little is known of Lindy's later career, but Cricket, Celia Mauri, lived in Neffs, Ohio.

Lindy and Cricket

Uncle Jack and Mary Lou (surnames unknown) came from the respective small southeast Ohio towns of Buchtel and Patriot. They worked at the *Jamboree* in 1936 and later at other radio outlets in Pennsylvania, including WEEU Reading in 1941, and had at least two Peer-Southern songbooks.

Ernest E. "Jimmy" Walker (1915–1990) had a much-traveled career, including stints in Los Angeles, the *Grand Ole Opry*, the *Midwestern Hayride*, Pittsburgh, and at least two in the *Jamboree*. Perhaps his greatest claim to fame was having the first recording of the country standard "Detour" in 1945. After retirement, he returned to his birthplace in Mason County, West Virginia. This photograph is from the early to mid-1940s.

Frank Dudgeon (1901–1987), the "West Virginia Mountain Boy," was a familiar figure at WWVA and other regional radio locales such as Fairmont, Columbus, Zanesville, and, briefly, Little Rock, Arkansas. In 1932 and 1933, he recorded eight songs for Champion and six numbers in 1947 for his own Frank's Folk Tunes.

Ray "Quarantine" Brown (1909–1981), a *Jamboree* comedian in the late 1930s, was nicknamed "the Ugliest Man in Radio." During this time, he worked in various units, including those of Jake Taylor and Cowboy Loye. In his autobiography, Grandpa Jones recalled that the only time anyone accused "Quarantine" of looking good was once when he was holding a chocolate cake that wound up in his face after being in a car wreck.

Millie Wayne (1920–1990) and Bonnie Baldwin (1924–2008) gained popularity as the Radio Rangerettes. Millie, on the left, was a McKeesport, Pennsylvania, native and sister of Curley Miller. She left WWVA in 1952 and worked for a time at a McKeesport bank. Leaving music a few years later, Bonnie remained active in the Wheeling-Bridgeport region until the 1990s. (Williams family collection.)

James Conwell, stage name "Slim Carter" (1917–1976) and wife "Brown Eyes" (1921–1985) divided the 1940s between WWVA, WKST New Castle, Pennsylvania, and other stations. The two published song booklets, and Slim recorded for MGM in 1949 and 1950, specializing in songs like "A Penny Postcard" and "Hungry Heart." (Williams family collection.)

Through the mid-1950s, WWVA radio had daily country music shows in quarter- and half-hour segments beginning at 4:30 a.m. Pictured here is a 1945 daily schedule as printed on the reverse side of a card-sized photograph of the *Jamboree* cast when it was a studio presentation. Times when there are no shows were for news and/or network programs.

WWVA
Hillbilly Program Schedule

4:30	Toby Stroud
5:00	Davis Twins
5:30	Chuckwagon Gang
6:00	Reed Dunn
6:15	Radio Rangerettes
7:30	Toby Stroud
9:15	Sunflower and Paul
1:30	Toby Stroud
1:45	Newcomer Twins
2:00	Gay Schwing's Gang
2:15	Radio Rangerettes
2:30	Rangers Quartet
2:45	Reed Dunn
3:00	Sunflower and Paul
4:15	Chuckwagon Gang
4:45	Davis Twins
11:30	Rangers Quartet
12:00	Chuckwagon Gang
12:30	Gay Schwing's Gang

1170 On Your Dial

Joe Barker (1914–1985) and his wife, Little Shirley Riggs (1916–1995), were *Jamboree* favorites from 1938 until they split in 1951, with time out for Joe being in service during World War II. Their touring group usually bore the name Chuckwagon Gang, although, during the 1939 *Jamboree* Goodwill Tour, it took the name of Joe Barker's Radio Circus.

The Chuckwagon Ploughboys represented an amalgam of Curley Miller's Ploughboys and Joe Barker's Chuckwagon Gang, organized for one single weeklong tour. From left to right are (first row) Jimmy Hutchison, Shirley Barker, and Sonny Day; (second row) Joe Barker, "Willie Whistle" (William McIlvane), Smilie Sutter, and Curley Miller.

Gay Schwing (1904–1983), daughter Ramona (1929–?), and brother Herman (1914–1985) and their Gang from the Hills were a popular *Jamboree* act in the late 1940s. Gay was an earlier band member of Fred Craddock's Happy Five. Fiddler Flavil Miller (not pictured here), who married Ramona, is the only surviving member of the band. (William family collection.)

Pennsylvania-born Mervin Shiner (b. 1921) is best known for having the original gold record for the children's Easter song, "Peter Cottontail" in 1950. His career goes back to the late 1930s, performing with his mother. He spent some time as a *Jamboree* regular in the 1950s. At age 99, he is still picking and singing. (Dave Sichak collection.)

William "Mack" Jeffers (1898–?) led a band called the Fiddlin' Farmers at WWVA and then WMMN in the early 1940s. He returned to his Tennessee homeland after the war, but son Sleepy (1922–1992) returned to the *Jamboree*, as did Shorty Godwin, who worked as comic "Hiram Hayseed" in the Border Riders from 1947 until he died in 1959.

Billed as "Radio's Only Blind Twins," Eileen (1925–1981) and Maxine (1925–1990), the Newcomer Twins, were a popular WWVA team from 1942 to 1948. One of their publicity shots pictured them in front of a mirror, giving the false impression that they were quadruplets. (Terrence McGill collection.)

Lew Childre (1901–1961), the "Man from Alabam," was sometimes called "Dr. Lew" because of his early work with medicine shows. He established himself as a favorite for three years at WWVA (1939–1942) and later at the *Grand Ole Opry*. During his *Jamboree* days, he sometimes used for support Floyd and Marge Tillman, a threesome called the Buckeyes, Bill Jones, and a trained dog named "Mr. Pooch."

The cast of the *Jamboree* for 1939 is seated behind a representation of the three states that join near the Wheeling area: Ohio, Pennsylvania, and West Virginia.

Two

THE GOLDEN YEARS
1946–1962

A 1946 Hollywood film entitled *The Best Years of Our Lives* became a reality for WWVA fans and viewers. The *Jamboree*'s grand reopening at the Virginia Theater helped usher in what is now considered the classic era of country music. Artists like Doc Williams and his band, now augmented with winsome wife Chickie, and Big Slim were in their musical prime. So, too, were Joe and Shirley Barker with their Chuckwagon Gang (not the gospel music legends), while newcomers that became legendary included versatile country vocalist Hawkshaw Hawkins, Ramblin' Roy Scott, and the husband-wife teams of Wilma Lee and Stoney Cooper and Lee and Juanita Moore. Earlier WWVA management had not encouraged their musicians to make records, but times changed, as both the Coopers and Hawkins had their records played by country deejays all over the United States. Those of Doc and Chickie had only regional airplay, and those of the Moores had quite limited distribution. Scott had one release on MGM and a few on small labels. The Barkers split in 1950 and never did record.

Roughly during the middle of this era, 1953–1958, the CBS Radio network broadcasted a portion of the program, alternating with other barn dance programs in such locales as Shreveport, Dallas, Knoxville, and Richmond. Although network radio was in decline, the affiliation apparently did provide a boost. Meanwhile, others joined the cast, most notably the young vocalist Dusty Owens, Maybelle Seiger, Hardrock Gunter, the Osborne Brothers, the Maine-born team of Lone Pine (Hal Breau) and Betty Cody, and the all-female Abbie Neal and her Ranch Girls, who eventually moved to the casino-club circuit in Las Vegas and Reno. Although rockabilly influences made some dent on the country scene, the *Jamboree*, as well as the music, survived nearly intact.

Other barn dance programs were facing uncertain futures. *The National Barn Dance* from WLS Chicago closed in 1960, although it soon revived on a limited basis at WGN for another five years. Richmond's *Old Dominion Barn Dance* briefly revived as the *New Dominion Barn Dance*. *The Louisiana Hayride* and *The Big D Jamboree* ran into road bumps. Television took the biggest toll on these programs. For the *Jamboree*, the major threat came from the closing and demolition of the Virginia Theater in July 1962. However, the show reopened the next week a block away in the Rex Theater, although problems remained to be solved.

Norman "Bud" Messner (1917–2001), a Virginia native and Pennsylvania resident, led a band called the Skyliners that were *Jamboree* regulars for some years in the mid-1950s. During that time, Messner usually played bass and sang duets with his then-wife, Molly Darr (c. 1928–2007). Mandolin picker Bill Bailey was a noted band member. Messner once said his three ambitions were to appear on the *Grand Ole Opry* (apparently once), to work the *Jamboree* (regularly for some years), and to own an NBC radio station, which he did—WSCG in Chambersburg, Pennsylvania. The illustration at left pictures the couple, while the one below shows him as a station owner.

During their decade at the *Jamboree* (1947–1957), the Coopers ranked among the most memorable and popular in the program's history. They are pictured about 1951 with Clan members Will Carver on resonator guitar; Abner Cole on bass and comedy; Wilma Lee, vocal and guitar; and Stoney Cooper on fiddle and vocal. In addition, Stoney is in the circle. (Terrence McGill collection.)

In the *Jamboree's* first three decades, most musical groups carried a comedian, partly because they played numerous shows in schools. Hawkshaw Hawkins, in the early 1950s, had a comic known as "Fireball." The identity of Fireball is unknown, although he bears some resemblance to Slim Mays, who had worked at WMMN Fairmont in 1941. (George Hausser collection.)

Abbie Neal (1918–2004) was born Esther McKinnon. She was a fiddler who first came to WWVA as a member of Cowboy Phil and His Golden West Girls. She later left and organized her own Ranch Girls western band that attained not only several years of *Jamboree* popularity during the 1950s, but also weekly television programs in Wheeling, Pittsburgh, and Johnstown. Later, she and the Ranch Girls went to Nevada and played the clubs in Reno and Las Vegas. She recorded sparingly for both Admiral and Wheeling. (Williams family collection.)

Cherokee Sue (1922–1967) and Little John Graham (1920–2008) were one of the Mountain State's most beloved musical couples. However, their stay at WWVA and the *Jamboree* lasted only a few months in 1950. John credited this to the fact that their time slot on the daily morning shows came too early to attract a wide audience, so they returned to WPDX Clarksburg. They are pictured here with John Jr., who started first grade at the elementary school on Wheeling Island.

Mississippi-born fiddler Buddy Durham (1920–2005) spent a decade at the *Jamboree* from 1954, not only displaying his skills on his instrument of choice. He and his wife, Marion, also frequently sang duets on the program. During his years at WWVA, Durham recorded numerous tunes on the Emperor label, sometimes altering the titles slightly, such as changing "Mississippi Sawyer" to "Mississippi Sawmill." (Williams family collection.)

From the mid-1950s, Wilma Lee and Stoney Cooper were joined at the *Jamboree* by attractive teenage daughter Carol Lee. She married Hank Snow's son Jimmie Rodgers Snow and performed gospel duets as part of his ministry, recording on the Heart Warming label. After their divorce, she led the Carol Lee Singers as an *Opry* vocal backup group. (Richard Weize and More Bears Archive.)

Country music's most celebrated brother duet of the 1947–1964 era, Ira and Charlie Louvin (born Loudermilk), had a short career at the *Jamboree* in the fall of 1957. According to the recollections of Sonny Osborne, Ira threw a temper-tantrum when he learned that his portion of the *Jamboree* had been preempted by a University of Pittsburgh football game. The Louvins soon returned to the *Grand Ole Opry*.

One of the all-time *Jamboree* greats, Huntington native Harold "Hawkshaw Hawkins (1921–1963), first used a band during his 1946–1953 years at WWVA. The Nighthawks are, from left to right (kneeling) Red Watkins; (standing) steel player Jiggs Lemley, Bud Nelson, Hawkins, and fiddler Glen Ferguson. Pictured elsewhere in this book is his comedian Fireball. (Richard Weize and More Bears Archive.)

Harold "Hawkshaw" Hawkins came to the *Jamboree* in 1946 following distinguished service in World War II and brief radio work in New Castle, Pennsylvania. He went on to become one of WWVA's best-known stars before moving on to the *Ozark Jubilee* in 1953 and the *Grand Ole Opry* in 1954. This is apparently his first professional photograph. (John Morris collection.)

HAWKSHAW HAWKINS
"Forty Yards of Personality"

Almost simultaneously with his *Jamboree* years, Hawkshaw Hawkins became one of the better sellers in the King Records country division, recording over 90 songs for the company by 1953. He moved on to RCA Victor and Columbia later but returned to King in 1962 for his final session, which included his biggest hit "Lonesome 7-7203." (Richard Weize and More Bears Archive.)

Byesville, Ohio, native Toby Stroud (1921–1996) at times worked both solo and with his Blue Mountain Boys, first coming to WWVA in 1944. Stroud recorded for Decca and MGM and also worked at the WRVA *Old Dominion Barn Dance* in Richmond. (Williams family collection.)

While there are many photographs of Doc Williams and his band, this one from 1950 is perhaps the most representative. Pictured from left to right are comedian William H. "Hiram Hayseed" Godwin; fiddler Cy Williams; vocalist and occasional bass player Chickie Williams; accordionist Marion Martin; and guitar and vocal, Doc himself. This band remained intact until Godwin's death in 1959.

Joe Barker (1914–1985) and his wife, Little Shirley (1916–1995), led a band usually known as the Chuckwagon Gang at WWVA from 1938 until they broke up about 1951.

Happy-Go-Lucky Joe Barker, who had worked solo prior to his 1938 marriage to Little Shirley, stayed as a solo act although he subsequently departed from the *Jamboree* and performed on a variety of radio stations as vocalist and deejay. He spent most of the 1960s and 1970s singing and spinning records at WBUC in Buckhannon, West Virginia.

Mandolinist Charles (1916–2004) and guitarist Danny (1919–2004), the Bailey Brothers, made the transition from old-time duet to full bluegrass bandleaders in the early 1950s with the help of fiddler Clarence "Tater" Tate and bass player Jake Tullock. Natives of East Tennessee, the band came to Wheeling for a two-year stint in May 1952. Although this photograph shows them in front of a WPTF Raleigh microphone, the autographs are signed WWVA. Danny later worked many years for Cas Walker in Knoxville. (Terrence McGill collection.)

Granada, Mississippi, native Will Carver remains best known as a longtime band member for Wilma Lee and Stoney Cooper, including their 1947–1957 decade at the *Jamboree*. An expert on mandolin, resonator, and steel guitar in addition to fiddle, Carver recorded many numbers with them and even cut a few discs on his own. (Terrence McGill collection.)

Big Slim, the Lone Cowboy, well known for his love of and training of horses, was apparently almost equally known for his canine pals. This photograph, shot around 1946 by a fence where other *Jamboree* stars were also pictured, shows Big Slim with one of "man's best friends." To date, no shots of Slim with a cat have surfaced. (Terrence McGill collection.)

BIG SLIM
"The Lone Cowboy"

BIG SLIM — "The Lone Cowboy"

Big Slim, the Lone Cowboy, was almost as well known as a horse trainer as he had been as an entertainer. In the warmer months, he often used trained horses in his show and did rope and whip tricks as well. (Williams family collection.)

49

Reed Dunn (1918–2002), known as "the Singing Mountaineer," was a popular *Jamboree* regular in the later 1940s. His style bore some similarity to the better-known Bradley Kinkaid and sometimes had a humorous touch. In keeping with a stereotypical mountaineer image, he is often pictured with guitar and gun as stage props. He also worked for police departments in Wheeling suburbs and later retired to Florida. (John Morris collection.)

Henry "Redd" Stewart (1921–2003) is best known for his composition of such songs as "Tennessee Waltz" and "Soldier's Last Letter" as well as fiddling and singing with Pee Wee King's Golden West Cowboys. But he sometimes went on his own, including a stint on Chicago television and with the *Jamboree*. (Williams family collection.)

Live photographs from the *Jamboree* are uncommon. This one-of-a-kind snapshot shows the Osborne Brothers in action with one of Red Allen's successors, Jimmy Brown. (Terrence McGill collection.)

Another live-on-stage, one-of-a-kind snapshot features an unlikely twosome. On the left is Kenny Roberts, best remembered as a great yodeler (but not that much of a cowboy), with bluegrass legend Jimmy Martin (1927–2005), who led his Sunny Mountain Boys at the *Jamboree* in the early 1960s. (Terrence McGill collection.)

Of the various brother teams that worked with Red Belcher's Cumberland Ridge Runners, none was more celebrated or fondly remembered than Everett and Bea, the Lilly Brothers. The Raleigh County, West Virginia, natives became best known for their role as bluegrass pioneers in New England. With Don Stover, they were inducted into the Bluegrass Hall of Honor. (Terrence McGill collection.)

Everett and Bea Lilly apparently either owned or drove the stretch limo that transported themselves and other WWVA entertainers to their personal appearances. With the bus parked on Wheeling Island, they posed for this photograph about 1949; Everett is holding the mandolin and Bea the guitar. This is about the time they cut their first records on the Page label.

Jimmie Williams (1930–1985) was born in Hamilton, Ohio, and was musically active in southwest Ohio on both radio and television. He recorded for both MGM and smaller labels. In addition, he appeared in the mid-1950s photographs as a *Jamboree* regular. Since his name is a rather common one, further information on his career has been virtually impossible to trace.

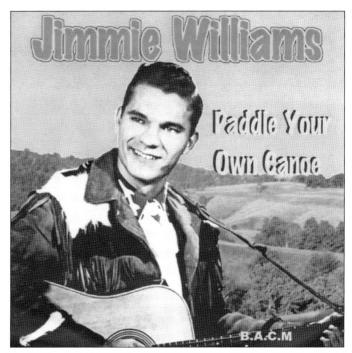

Pictured is another lineup of Wilma Lee and Stoney Cooper and the Clinch Mountain Clan during their *Jamboree* years. This one features, from left to right, Will Carver (resonator guitar), Stoney Cooper (fiddle), Wilma Lee Cooper (guitar), Blaine Stewart (mandolin), and Dapper Dan Martin (bass fiddle and comedy). (Williams family collection.)

Missouri-born Dusty Owens (1930–2015) was a *Jamboree* bright spot during the mid-1950s days of the CBS network affiliation. With a sharp band containing young fiddle genius Buddy Spicher, Donna Darlene, and veteran comic Lazy Jim Day and a Columbia Records contract, Owens made a big if brief splash on the country scene. His song "Once More" has become a true classic. He later settled in Florida as an Amway Corporation executive. (Both, Williams family collection.)

Bill Bailey was a well-known mandolin picker who worked with various bands at WWVA Wheeling, WRVA Richmond, and other radio locales. His work at the *Jamboree* included sideman stints with both Toby Stroud and Bud Messner. (Terrence McGill collection.)

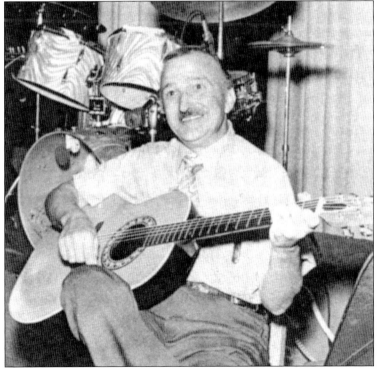

Ray "Abner Doolittle" Couture (1919–2012) had a long career with the *Jamboree* and WWVA beginning in 1952. As a band member, he worked with Lone Pine and Betty Cody and also Hawkshaw Hawkins. From 1954 until 1961, he led the staff band and later worked as an assistant director behind the scenes and as an accountant for WWVA. He also wrote songs for both Lone Pine and Betty Cody and later for Doc and Chickie Williams. (Dave Heath collection.)

The Kershaw Brothers—Rusty (1938–2001) and Doug (b. 1936)—were a unique twosome who combined Cajun-flavored harmony duets with rockabilly. The Louisiana-born brothers spent only a year at the *Jamboree* (1957–1958). Their original song "Louisiana Man" has become a country standard, and "Diggy Liggy Lo" has been known to be sung by Bedouin youth in the Sinai Desert. Rusty retired from music in the 1960s, but Doug continued with his unique form of Cajun country into the 21st century. (Williams family collection.)

Harold "Lone Pine" Breau (1916–1977) and his wife, Betty, ranked second only to Dick Curless among New England country musicians. His *Jamboree* years pretty much coincided with the program's time on network radio. Many of his songs extolled the beauty of New England and the Maritimes such as "Prince Edward Island Is Heaven to Me," "Coast of Maine," and "Apple Blossom Time in Annapolis Valley." (Richard Weize and More Bears Archive.)

Rita Cote (1921–2005) was a Maine-born French-Canadian girl who married Hal "Lone Pine" Breau in 1940 and sang duets with him as well as her own solos until they split in 1959. Her best-known songs on RCA Victor were the answer song "I Found Out More than You Ever Knew" and "Tom-Tom Yodel." She ultimately retired to Auburn, Maine. (Richard Weize and More Bears Archive.)

Lone Pine and Betty Cody—new WWVA artists at the time—are pictured on this calendar for 1953. Also pictured are their two sons Lenny and Dennis, both musicians in their own right. Lenny grew up to become one of the great guitarists in history. Sadly, he also became a homicide victim in a case that remains unsolved. (Williams family collection.)

Gene Hooper (1923–2010), a native of the ultimate Down East locale Machias, Maine, worked as a *Jamboree* regular in the mid-1950s. He and Hal "Lone Pine" Breau married respective sisters Betty Cody and "Little Flo." A longtime spokesman for traditional country music in New England as well as a deejay, Hooper recorded for the Canadian Arc label and the Wheeling-based Doxx Company. (Williams family collection.)

Bonnie Baldwin (1924–2008), a longtime resident of Bridgeport, Ohio, worked off and on at the *Jamboree* for decades. She was Millie Wayne's Radio Rangerette duet partner during World War II. Later, she became a solo artist in the mid-1950s (as pictured), worked on children's television in Steubenville, and appeared on many WWVA reunion shows. Although Baldwin made numerous recordings, she never had the one that would propel her to major stardom.

Early members of the Sunshine Boys, Smitty (1916–1986) and Tennessee (1918–2009), the Smith Brothers, spent most of their musical careers in Georgia. But from 1960 to 1962, they worked weekday television in Pittsburgh with Slim Bryant's Wildcats and Saturday nights at the *Jamboree*. Recording for Mercury, Sing, and especially Capitol, they are perhaps best known today for such technology-themed sacred songs as "God's Rocket Ship" and "Working in God's Factory."

Don Kidwell worked at the *Jamboree* in the late 1940s and at the *Brush Creek Follies* at KMBC in the early 1950s and recorded a total of 10 sides for Mercury and MGM. While at Wheeling, Doc Williams stimulated his interest in aviation, and Kidwell eventually spent 27 years as a pilot for Pan American Airways. He is now deceased.

Before Hank Snow attained major stardom in the 1950s, he spent six months at the *Jamboree* in 1946 and later gained additional experience at WFIL Philadelphia. During his WWVA days, he was closely associated with Big Slim and actually recorded his "Sunny Side of the Mountain" on RCA Canada first. Then, in 1950, he had major hits with "I'm Movin' On" and "The Golden Rocket," and the rest is history. (Williams family collection.)

When Abbie Neal left Cowboy Phil Reed to form her own Ranch Girls band, the other two girls, Gay and Tina Franzi, remained with their leader. They, too, eventually left Phil and were, in turn, replaced by the McCumbee Sisters. By 1972, both Gay (Steere) and Tina (Carlton) had left show business and resided only a few blocks apart in Cleveland. (Williams family collection.)

Jamboree comedy skits in the 1940s could sometimes become rather complex and involved. This one featured a cast of, from left to right, (first row) Hawkshaw Hawkins, Jiggs Lemley, Shirley Barker, Sleepy Jeffers, Shorty Godwin, and Nial "Sonny" Davis; (second row) Curley Miller. Sadly, the script has not survived. (Williams family collection.)

Monty Blake (1922–2008), born John Monto, was a memorable accordion player like Marion Martin and wore many hats over the decades at the *Jamboree*. He worked in a variety of positions in a long life in Wheeling: sideman, soloist, staff band member, leader, and eventually stage manager, all of which earned him a space in the 1983 Walkway of Stars outside the Capitol Theater. (Williams family collection.)

Dusty Shaver (1925–1982) specialized in humorous songs and also played a comedic role as Oscar Quiddlemurp. He was on the *Jamboree* in 1947 but spent more of his career in Fairmont and Clarksburg, where he played a similar role, first working with Buddy Starcher and then Cherokee Sue and Little John Graham. In later years, Shaver worked as a radio deejay in Oakland, Maryland.

The Hal Camp band joined the *Jamboree* in 1954, displaying considerable diversity. The personnel were, from left to right, Hal Camp; his wife, Vickie Lee; Bud Kilgore; and Curley Holiday. The latter, a lead vocalist, had a separate contract with King Records, although his career with that label proved to be rather short.

Skeeter Bonn (1923–1994, standing at left), the stage name for Junior Broughn, spent several years at the *National Barn Dance*, *Midwestern Hayride*, and finally at the *Jamboree*, during which time he also recorded for RCA Victor and Admiral Records. One of the few country singers to come to prominence after World War II to yodel, his specialty numbers included songs like "The Yodeling Bird" and "Yodeling Man" and more conventional numbers like "Honey Baby."

MAYBELLE SEIGER and The Sons of The Plains, WWVA Wheeling, W. Va.

Pennsylvania native Maybelle Seiger (1923–1999) was another *Jamboree* stalwart through the mid-1950s. She also had a contract with RCA Victor's "X" records. One of her more memorable songs reflecting her own background was "Sleepy Susquehanna Waltz" and also "The Lighthouse on the Hill." Maybelle Seiger also worked with her band, the Sons of the Plains, which was led by her husband, John Henry (Curley), and featured the Cook Brothers. In the 1980s, she appeared at some WWVA reunions. (Williams family collection.)

Finley "Red" Belcher (1914–1952) was a clawhammer banjoist who often worked with brother acts while excelling as a "pitchman," effective as an on-the-air salesman. Those who worked with him included the Mayse, Hankinson, Richey, and Lilly Brothers as well as Roy Scott. Before going on his own, Belcher worked with Buddy Starcher. He recorded sparingly on the Page label and was killed in an auto accident. (Terrence McGill collection.)

Abbie Neal (1918–2004), a member of Cowboy Phil's Golden West Girls and longtime leader of the Ranch Girls, was quite popular in her native Pennsylvania, where she had programs on local television, eventually going to Nevada more or less permanently. Her image was captured by a fan at one of the many unnamed Keystone State's country music parks. (Terrence McGill collection.)

Flavil "Flannels" Miller (b. 1930) fiddled with both Doc Williams's Border Riders and Gay Schwing and the Gang from the Hills in the mid-1940s, marrying Schwing's daughter Ramona. Afterward, he became a United Brethren minister. Following retirement, he renewed his interest in the fiddle, cut two fiddle albums, and worked in a band called the Get Along Gang. An accompanist is behind him.

WILLIAM H. GODWIN

William H. "Shorty" Godwin (1889–1959), also known as "Hiram Hayseed," was a vaudeville veteran who worked first at WWVA and WMMN with the Fiddlin' Farmers. After the war, he spent about a dozen years with Doc Williams's Border Riders. His specialty was playing fiddle and singing humorous songs such as "Sally Sweet," "Shirts," and "Ridin' a Humpback Mule."

Chickie Williams (1919–2007) did not become a Border Rider until after World War II. In 1947, her successful recording of "Beyond the Sunset" elevated her to *Jamboree* star status equal to that of her husband, Doc. This circumstance continued until a stroke ended her performing career some years prior to her death. She recorded many classics such as "Wintertime in Maine" and "World's Meanest Mother." (John Morris collection.)

Marion Keyoski, known professionally as Marion Martin (1919–1990), was a noted blind accordion player, most famous for his long years with Doc Williams's Border Riders. Martin also worked at WIBC Indianapolis. He was with Doc from 1946 through the 1980s as well as recording two long-play albums. (Williams family collection.)

Abbie Neal's Ranch Girls were among the most popular all-girl country western groups in the 1950s in their WWVA and Pennsylvania-television listening area, where they were managed by Abbie's husband, Gene Johnson. Later, they repeated their popularity in the Nevada nightclub and casino circuit. Unfortunately, the identity of each girl in the photograph is now unknown, but all were quite talented. (Williams family collection.)

A radio veteran, Cowboy Phil Reed (c. 1911–1977) came to WWVA with a threesome known as the Golden West Girls, made up of Abbie Neal and Gay and Tina Franzi. Neal later left to form her Ranch Girls. Gay and Tina remained longer, recording on Bibletone. Later, Phil left and did deejay work at WHJB in Greensburg, Pennsylvania. (Williams family collection.)

The Sunshine Boys hailed from the Atlanta area and were a highly popular and versatile gospel quartet, who came to WWVA in 1949 and remained for about three years. Pictured are, from left to right, (at piano) Eddie Wallace (1924–2014); standing J.D. Sumner (1924–1998), Milton "Ace" Richman (1916–1999), and Fred Daniel (1925–2007). In addition to extensive radio work, they even made western movies with Charles Starrett and Eddie Dean. (Williams family collection.)

In addition to their legendary status in gospel quartet circles attained in Atlanta and Wheeling, the Sunshine Boys made a name for themselves in Hollywood B-Western movies. Over the years, they journeyed to California, where they sang and doubled as either cowhands or posse members for Eddie Dean, Lash Larue, and most often Charles Starrett (also known as the Durango Kid). Pictured are two stills from the latter's Columbia films. Pictured above are, from left to right, Ace Richman, Fred Daniel, Smiley Burnette, Eddie Wallace, and J.D. Sumner. Below are, from left to right, Fred Daniel, Eddie Wallace, J.D. Sumner, Ace Richman, and Charles Starrett (as Durango).

Jamboree staff bands were periodically reshuffled as membership changed, and often, names of the band changed as well. This group from 1952 was led by Roy Scott (second row, center). Other members included, from left to right, Gene Jenkins (guitar), Monty Blake (accordion), and Will Carver (fiddle). (Williams family collection.)

Pete Cassell (1917–1954), well known in radio circles as "the Blind Minstrel," achieved his peak popularity at WWVA and at a variety of Atlanta stations. Cassell's *Jamboree* stays came in 1940 and for a longer stretch beginning in 1945. He won the show's popularity contest in 1946. Cassell specialized in songs like "Oh, How I Miss You" and recitations such as "Too Many Parties and Too Many Pals." (John Morris collection.)

Before they split in 1960, Lee and Juanita Moore ranked as one of country music radio's most popular husband-wife duets. They had been known as such for a decade before coming to WWVA in 1950. Sadly, the few recordings they made together were all on the Cross Country label beginning in 1953. Memorable among them are "Paradise Valley" and "The Lord Is My Shepherd," an adaptation of the 23rd Psalm. (Terrence McGill collection.)

Walter "Lee" Moore (1914–1997) began his radio vocalist career about 1936, working at various stations until coming to WWVA in 1950. Through the 1940s and 1950s, he often worked as a duet with his first wife, Juanita. When their marriage dissolved, he continued at the *Jamboree* into the 1970s but was almost as well-known as the all-night "Coffee Drinkin' Night Hawk" deejay. He recorded extensively on small labels and ultimately retired to Wynantskill, New York.

Millie Wayne (1919–1990) was an attractive brunette whose surname was Miller; she was the younger sister of *Jamboree* artist Curley Miller. At WWVA, she was half of the Radio Rangerettes with Bonnie Baldwin and also did some solo work. She recorded but sparingly, two sides for Cozy and a Rangerettes reunion album with Bonnie in the early 1960s. Millie Wayne spent her later working years at a bank in McKeesport, Pennsylvania.

Over its 72-year existence at WWVA, the *Jamboree* served as home base for numerous New Englanders. The four pictured here are, from left to right, "Crazy Elmer," Fiddlin' Harold Carter, Gene Hooper, and Ray Couture. Couture and Crazy Elmer spent most of their working careers there while Carter was a sideman with Lone Pine, Betty Cody, and Hooper. (Dave Heath collection.)

Ernest "Jimmy" Walker (1915–1990) came back from California to WWVA in 1949 and soon signed a contract with independent Intro Records. With them, he cut such quality numbers as "Loving Country Heart" and "High Geared Daddy." "Chetty," to whom this and other photographs in this book were addressed, worked in the mail room at WWVA. (Williams family collection.)

Jimmy Martin (1927–2005), one-time Bill Monroe protégé and self-styled "King of Bluegrass," spent nearly three years (January 1960–December 1962) at the *Jamboree*. In 17 years with Decca/MCA Records, he recorded 139 numbers with his Sunny Mountain Boys, many of them classics. Many critics consider his Wheeling years the musical peak of his career. Behind Martin are, from left to right, Paul Williams, Johnny Dacus, and J.D. Crowe. (Williams family collection.)

Donna Darlene (1938–2017) worked at the *Jamboree* in the mid-1950s with Dusty Owens and other acts. Once married to Cajun musician Doug Kershaw, in later years she settled in Nashville and married steel guitar and Dobro player Shot Jackson, the inventor of the ShoBro and ShoBud guitars. (John Morris collection.)

Sidney "Hardrock" Gunter (1925–2013) became known for his song "Birmingham Bounce." A veteran of World War II and Korea, serving on the staff of Gen. James Hartinger, Gunter came to WWVA in 1954 and worked for years as deejay, announcer, and vocalist. With Lee Sutton, he operated Essgee Records, preserving the music of several *Jamboree* artists. Moving to Colorado, he owned an insurance agency and gained belated recognition as a rockabilly pioneer. (Williams family collection.)

Originally known as yodeling vocalist Smilie (or Smiley) Sutter (1915–1980), after World War II he became more and more comic "Crazy Elmer." As one character or another, the man really named Anthony Slater put in about four decades as a much loved *Jamboree* entertainer. (Both, Williams family collection.)

Lois Johnson (1942–2014) and her husband, Kirk Hanserd, were *Jamboree* regulars in the late 1950s and early 1960s, often participating in tours with Jimmy Martin and the Sunny Mountain Boys. After going to Nashville, she signed with MGM and made several recordings in duet with Hank Williams Jr. She also made solo numbers, including a top-10 hit with "Loving You Would Never Grow Old" in 1974. (Williams family collection.)

Throughout the decade of the 1950s, Saturday night was *Jamboree* night for thousands and thousands of listeners. With television still in its infancy, the radio remained the source of entertainment for most rural Americans. Indeed, the *Jamboree* entertained many Canadian listeners as well. The signal extended as far as Newfoundland. Wheeling became a location where a family would scrimp and save to visit for that rare vacation, and seeing a live show on the stage was a dream of many. If they got there, this is what they saw.

Three

DECLINE AND REJUVENATION
1962–1970

In addition to the decline of big-time radio and competition from television, the biggest short-term problem facing the *Jamboree*'s future came from the small size of the Rex Theater, which seated only about 900 persons. Without more seats, one could hardly sell enough tickets to guarantee financial solvency. According to Barbara Smik, the principal advocates for maintaining the tradition came from her father, Doc Williams, and announcer-deejays John Corrigan and Lee Sutton. Doc and his band were touring extensively and were no longer on the program every week. Lee Moore did the Saturday night show and gained a large following as the all-night deejay nicknamed the "Coffee Drinkin' Night Hawk." Big Slim remained a regular and toured extensively, although his health became increasingly precarious. Hardrock Gunter also did deejay work. Fiddler Buddy Durham and his wife, Marion, did instrumentals and country duets. Roy Scott played the *Jamboree* on Saturdays and did deejay work in Pittsburgh as did a returning former regular, Jimmy Walker.

The turnaround came when executive Emil Mogul hired veteran vocalist Mac Wiseman as manager and sometime artist. Wiseman soon found a larger venue—the Wheeling Island Exhibition Hall—that could easily accommodate four-figure crowds and developed a relatively inexpensive monthly guest star system usually featuring big-name stars from the *Grand Ole Opry* or figures such as Johnny Cash, Buck Owens, or George Jones. Crowds swelled at least part of the time, and fiscal responsibility returned. Some new acts came on board such as Bob Gallion, Patti Powell, and Esco Hankins as well as bluegrass bands such as those of Red Smiley, Jim Greer, and Jim Eanes and guests like J.E. Mainer, a bona fide old-timer for whom Lee Sutton became a producer for a new set of his record albums.

Even more plans called for a return to their original home at the Capitol Theater. When Wiseman first came to WWVA, the station had become one of the few 50,000-watt all-country stations. By the name change in 1969 to *Jamboree USA*, when Wiseman returned to Nashville in 1970, the venerable barn dance was probably in better shape than it had been since the late 1950s.

Here is a 1962 cast photograph of the WWVA *Jamboree*. Pictured are, from left to right, (first row) Jimmy Nugent, Snook McFall, Roy Scott, George Adams, Skinny Clark, Bill McNett, Bob McNett, Dean McNett, Zeb Collins, Jimmy Martin, Paul Williams, and Bill Emerson; (second row) Lila Lou, Clyde Vogel, Buddy Durham, Hardrock Gunter, Jim Lowdermilk, George Mauersberger, Monty Blake, Lois Johnson, Kirk Hansert, Kathy Dee, Kenny Roberts, Norman Vaughn, and

John Corrigan; (third row) Crazy Elmer, Lee Sutton, Charles Hallman, George Hallman, Smokey Pleacher, Chickie Williams, Peeper Williams, Punkin Williams, Poochie Williams, Bill Guest, Marion Martin, Doc Williams, Ronnie Vandergrift, Donald Vandergrift, and Darrell Vandergrift. The location of this picture is uncertain, and a portion of this image appears on the front cover. (Williams family collection.)

In 1965, the New York radio executive Emil Mogul hired musician Mac Wiseman (1925–2019) to run the *Jamboree*, which had been losing ticket revenue. Wiseman moved the program to Wheeling Island, hired some new acts, sang, and instituted the monthly guest star system, which soon restored the *Jamboree* to profitability. He left in June 1970 for Nashville but left a wide mark. (Williams family collection.)

Kenny Biggs (d. 2005) was born in Sleepy Creek, West Virginia, and joined the cast of the *Jamboree* in 1960. He had at least three LPs to his credit as well as singles. Career highlights included the April 1972 Bahamas cruise with girl vocalist Jackie Smith, Gus and Jo Ann Thomas, and Lynn Stewart. He also toured military bases in Greenland and elsewhere. He worked as a deejay at WEEP in Pittsburgh. (Dave Heath collection.)

Jimmie Stephens (1929–2006) was born in Connecticut as James Papillo but anglicized his name for the stage. Jimmie had a soft voice reminiscent of pop vocalists. He joined the *Jamboree* in 1963, sometimes accompanied by his wife, Jo Ann Davis. Over the years, he recorded on such labels as Essgee, Stop, and Mark V. He toured the Northeast with an especially memorable show at the Thule Air Force Base in Greenland. (Dave Heath collection.)

Charles "Smokey" Pleacher (1918–1971) worked as a comedian with the Border Riders for a brief period in 1952 and again for about a dozen years after the death of Shorty Godwin. Over a long career, Doc Williams carried several quality comics in his band, but Smokey seems to have been his favorite. Pleacher also worked with other acts, including Wilma Lee and Stoney Cooper. (Williams family collection.)

George Adams (b. 1936) and Skinney Clark (1931–2001) worked as *Jamboree* regulars from 1962 until 1971 and sporadically thereafter. They were a fine country duet act and produced some high-quality honky-tonk music not only on the airwaves, but also in clubs in the Pittsburgh area. They often worked in a business owned by former Pittsburgh Pirate relief pitcher Elroy Face, who could sing credibly himself. (Williams family collection.)

George Kingsbury (1926–2012), professionally known as Kenny Roberts, could challenge Elton Britt as "King of the Yodelers" and had a long career in many locales. His radio popularity peaked at WLW Cincinnati 1948–1950, television at WHIO Dayton 1952–1957, and radio longevity at WWVA 1962–1975. National hits included "I Never See Maggie Alone," "Chocolate Ice Cream Cone," and "Billy and Nanny Goat," all of which had long popularity with children. (Williams family collection.)

Arkansas native James Britt Baker, known professionally as Elton Britt (1913–1972), became a *Jamboree* star in his later years, having begun a radio and recording career in the early 1930s with the original Beverly Hill Billies. Known initially for yodel songs like "Chime Bells," he attained his greatest fame for the World War II mega-hit "There's a Star Spangled Banner Waving Somewhere." He recorded extensively in later years for both RCA Victor and ABC Paramount and had his last noted hit with "The Jimmie Rodgers Blues" in 1968. He also appeared in three Western movies, two of them with Charles Starrett. He joined WWVA in 1969. (Williams family collection.)

One of the best new girl vocalists of the late 1960s was Kay Tolliver, who had a few years of *Jamboree* membership and a contract with Pappy Dailey's Musicor Records. She had some outstanding singles on the label typified by "man-bashing" song lyrics, such as "Your Own Medicine" and "I Don't Leave My Memory Anywhere." In mid-career, she had a name change to Kemmer via marriage but no charted records. (Williams family collection.)

Albany, Georgia, native Les Seevers joined the *Jamboree* in 1968. The next year he had his biggest hit, "What Kind of Magic," which spent nine weeks on the *Billboard* charts. Like many WWVA artists, Seever spent much of his professional career in Pennsylvania and once had a television show in Philadelphia. (Dave Heath collection.)

Tennessee-born Esco Hankins (1924–1990) spent most of his musical career on the radio in Knoxville and Lexington but was a *Jamboree* artist during his stay at the Wheeling Island Exhibition Hall in the mid-1960s. He had a voice and style not unlike that of Roy Acuff and did many covers of his hits on the King label, later moving to Mercury, Rem, Columbia, and Jewel. His best-known original was "Mother Left Me Her Bible."

Darnell Miller (b. 1937) has a *Jamboree* resume that began in 1966. A native of Bland, Virginia, and a veteran of Bluefield radio and television dating back to 1953, he celebrated his 50th anniversary in April 2017. Primarily a honky-tonk singer, Miller is probably best known for his tearjerker "Mommy, Will My Doggie Understand" and the honky-tonk "Hinges on the Door."

The Vandergrift Brothers came from Fairmont, worked as *Jamboree* regulars during the Wheeling Island Exhibition Hall years, and are remembered for their excellent harmony on either rockabilly songs or straight harmony. They recorded sparingly for Cozy and King. They are, from left to right, Darrell, Ron, and Don. (Williams family collection.)

Charlotte DeHaven (1948–2014) from Berkeley Springs first worked on the *Jamboree* under the name Penny Starr, making the charts at age 19. Going to Nashville in 1969, she took the name Penny DeHaven and made the *Billboard* listings 16 more times. But she never scored the really big hit.

Mary Lou Turner (b. 1947) was born in Hazard, Kentucky, moved to Dayton, Ohio, as a child. She joined the *Jamboree* in November 1965. During her nearly eight years at WWVA, she recorded both singles and an LP on the Jamboree USA label. Then with Jan Howard's departure from the *Bill Anderson Show*, she moved to Nashville, the *Grand Ole Opry*, and MCA Records, where she did both duets with her boss as well as solo chart makers. Later, in Branson, she spent several years with Boxcar Willie, recording on the Churchill label. During her years at Wheeling, she played many military bases. (Dave Heath collection.)

Moundsville native Kathleen Dearth (1933–1968) took the stage name "Kathy Dee," joined the *Jamboree* in the mid-1950s, and remained there off and on until her death. Along the way, she enjoyed a couple of chart makers with "Unkind Words" and "Don't Leave Me Lonely Too Long." However, eye problems led to blindness, and other issues contributed to her death at age 35.

Ramblin' Roy Scott (1926–2010), over the decades, proved to be a quality vocalist and lead guitarist, and also a fine fiddler when circumstances demanded. A *Jamboree* regular off and on from the late 1940s, he sang lead, led a band, and recorded sporadically with minor success, once remarking that his records were not "released but escaped." He had one release on MGM, but others were on smaller labels. (Williams family collection.)

Seeking a larger venue for the *Jamboree* home, management settled on the Exhibition Hall on Wheeling Island, which could easily accommodate twice the crowd size than the Rex Theater. The show was held there from January 1966 to mid-December 1969. The building was long and narrow, and the audience sat on folding chairs. Regulars presented a quality show, and the monthly guests included such stars as Bill Anderson, Connie Smith, and Buck Owens. Sadly, the historic but abandoned structure behind the current casino burned on New Year's Eve 2019. (Dave Heath collection.)

Four
CHANGING FOCUS
1971–1983

The return of the recently renamed *Jamboree USA* to its original home in the Capitol Theater (or Music Hall) at 1015 Main Street near the east end of the historic Wheeling Suspension Bridge, linking both Wheeling Island and the Buckeye State, inaugurated a new era of *Jamboree* history. Although radio had lost much of its audience from a generation earlier, the 50,000 watts of the "Friendly Voice of WWVA" still linked tens of thousands of country music fans in the northeastern USA and southeastern Canada to what was advertised as the "Wheeling Feeling" on Saturday nights. But the emphasis increasingly was turned toward the guest stars, with less attention toward the Saturday night regulars who now might appear on the show a dozen times a year or even less.

The monthly guest star system initiated by Mac Wiseman in 1966 to balance the *Jamboree* budget proved to be "just the tip of the proverbial iceberg." One did not have to be a financial wizard to see that Johnny Cash, Buck Owens, or Charlie Pride brought in more cash than the better known regular cast members such as Bob Gallion, Darnell Miller, or even Doc and Chickie Williams, although they took more cash with them when they departed. A national figure of lesser stature like Ronnie McDowell or John Conlee could still turn a profit although they did not pack them in like the superstars.

By the 1980s, the new system was nearly complete. An example from the latter half of 1983 illustrates the point. Twenty of the 25 Saturdays from late July were headlined by a guest star, most notably Loretta Lynn, Ray Price, and Tammy Wynette. Another show featured old-time *Jamboree* people from past years such as Doc and Chickie Williams and their daughters, Bill Jones, and Bonnie Baldwin. Regular performers were featured on three shows in December; one a salute to them, one on Christmas Eve, and another on New Year's Eve. In mid-October, the golden anniversary show took place. Other appearances by cast members came as opening acts for the guest stars.

Back in 1977, a July outdoor country music festival, Jamboree in the Hills, began some miles away as an annual outreach of the original program. It had been growing to mammoth proportions, attracting as many as 40,000 fans. Success was everywhere, yet many of the old traditions seemed lost in the shuffle.

Braxton County native Buddy Griffin (b. 1948) became proficient on stringed instruments, especially fiddle and banjo. He served on the *Jamboree* staff band in the early 1970s. In 1988, he recorded an album on which he played all the instruments. He founded the Bluegrass Degree Program at Glenville State College.

Patti Powell (b. 1937) and Bob Gallion (1929–1999) came to the *Jamboree* in 1969 and remained for nearly 20 years, each doing solos as well as duets. They also took over the talent agency after Mac Wiseman's departure in 1970. Their best-known duet was a classic cheating song, "Love by Appointment." Powell still lives on a farm near Quaker City, Ohio. (Williams family collection.)

From the late 1930s, *Jamboree* became known as a show where girl vocalists could gain more attention than on other barn dance programs. This continued into the 1970s when Holly Garrett (b. 1944), a young wife and mother, joined the regular cast. Garrett hailed from Fombell, Pennsylvania, and was a Mega Records contractee. She is fondly remembered for her winning personality. (Williams family collection.)

One of the most dynamic *Jamboree* regulars in the 1970s was Slim Lehart, who became known by his signature song, "The Wheeling Cat." A native of nearby Marshall County, Lehart had both talent and charisma, which he combined for exciting stage performances and delivering quality versions of such numbers as "Sidewalks of Chicago" and "Forever and Always." Lehart also served as a Marshall County commissioner and operated-entertained at the Slim Lehart Lounge in Wheeling.

The Heckels were a family group consisting of father William "Pee Wee" (1932–2008), son "Jay Bird," and daughters Susie (b. around 1956) and Beverly (b. around 1960). They achieved considerable attention in the late 1960s and early 1970s and even cracked the charts briefly on RCA Victor, by which time Pee Wee had been replaced by Susie's then-husband Denny Franks. Pictured below are, from left to right, Pee Wee Heckel; Jay Bird, Beverly, and Susan; Beverly had a brief solo career on RCA and married Johnny Russell in 1977. In more recent times, the sisters have divided their time between Arkansas and West Virginia. (Both, Williams family collection.)

Mississippi-born Johnny Russell (1940–2001) first gained attention as co-composer of the 1963 Buck Owens superhit "Act Naturally." Later signing with RCA, he joined the *Jamboree* cast in March 1972. From August 1972, he had a hit of his own with "Redneck, White Socks, and Blue Ribbon Beer." He later joined the *Opry*, where he also did comedy but often returned to play at Jamboree in the Hills.

Florida-born, Georgia-reared LaWanda Lindsey (b. 1953) made her first chart appearance at the age of 16, joining the *Jamboree* cast while still a teenager. Meeting Buck Owens's girl vocalist Susan Raye made a sufficient impression on LaWanda to leave the Chart label and WWVA for Capitol at 20 and score five more appearances in 1973 and 1974 for them; she later signed with Mercury. She retired in 1978. (Williams family collection.)

JO ANN and GUS THOMAS
JAMBOREE U.S.A., WHEELING, W.VA.

From 1968 until the mid-1970s, Gus (1939–1987) and Jo Ann Thomas were a popular team who also sang solos at the *Jamboree*. Gus was also a deejay and emcee. Among other achievements, he sang the last song at the Exhibition Hall in December 1969 and, a week later, the first one at the Capitol. Eventually, they returned to Pennsylvania, where Gus passed away a few years later. (Williams family collection.)

Skilled square dancers have long been a feature with radio and television barn dance programs. Of several groups who worked at the *Jamboree*, the Ohio Valley Clogghoppers from Bellaire, Ohio, are pictured here. (Williams family collection.)

Lynda Kaye Lance (b. 1949) came from Smithfield, Pennsylvania. She joined the *Jamboree* in 1970 and over a decade made the Billboard charts seven times on Royal American and other labels with "My Guy" rating highest at number 46. Afterward, she seems to have vanished from the country mainstream. (Williams family collection.)

The daughters of Doc and Chickie Williams often played on the *Jamboree*, although only Karen ever held actual membership. Barbara (b. 1940), Madeline (b. 1943), and Karen (b. 1944), known as "Chickie's Chicks" or "Peeper," "Poochie," and "Punkin," were closely associated with their parents in music, although all had professional careers in their own right. After their parents' retirement, the girls, as the Williams Sisters, recorded a quality sacred album. (Williams family collection.)

Karen "Punkin" McKenzie, the only one of Doc and Chickie Williams' daughters to opt for a musical career, held a separate *Jamboree* membership for several years from 1970. In addition to cutting some records with her parents and sisters, Karen made solo recordings for the Wheeling and ABC labels. Her oldest son, Andy, grew up to serve 12 years in the West Virginia Senate and as mayor of Wheeling. (Williams family collection.)

Charlie Pride (b. 1938), the first African American country music superstar, also set a new and unsurpassed *Jamboree USA* record on October 23, 1971, when more than 10,000 paid admissions packed into the Capitol for four shows (not all broadcast live on the air) to see him perform. Pride later returned in 1983 when he was honored on the Walkway of Stars.

The Blue Ridge Quarter also became *Jamboree* legends. Two versions of the group are shown here. The image at right dates from the 1960s, when Elmo Fagg was the leader. Fagg retired in 1969 and was replaced by LaVerne Tripp (below, top right). The latter was celebrated for his original lyrics set to older country tunes such as "I Know" (from "Sweeter than the Flowers") and "He's Coming Soon" (from "Ashes of Love"). Others are unidentified. Fred Daniel (not pictured) was also a noted member of the Blue Ridge Quartet and sometimes did solo work on the *Jamboree*. In 1980, the group made a live album on stage at the Capitol Music Hall. The quartet dissolved in 1985. (Right, Dave Heath collection; below, Williams family collection.)

New Generation Express

Lionel Cartwright (b. 1960) was born in Gallipolis, Ohio, but lived most of his youth in West Virginia, where he developed a wide variety of musical skills. While attending Wheeling College, he directed the staff band at the *Jamboree*. From 1982, he worked for the Nashville Network and, over a four-year period, had a dozen hits on MCA, including "Leap of Faith" and "I Watched It All on My Radio." Later, he composed television show themes, including one for Rachel Ray's program on the Food Network, and became involved in church work. Cartwright is pictured above, fourth from left, with the *Jamboree* band, the New Generation Express. Their album on the Rome label covered songs ranging from "Bye Bye Love" to White Lightning." Cartwright is also pictured at left. (Above, Dave Heath collection; left, Williams family collection.)

Jo Ann Davis married Jimmie Stephens—pictured here on the *Jamboree* stage—and they worked together as a duet. Their daughter Jomina also sang with them. After Stephens's death, Jo Ann married Ron Vandergrift and later became widowed. Davis still lives in the Wheeling area. (Jo Ann Davis collection.)

Dick Curless (1932–1996) is one of the more popular *Jamboree* figures of the early 1970s and the first to record a live album on stage for a major label, which he did on September 3, 1972. Probably the most significant New Englander in country music, Curless had numerous hits on the *Billboard* charts, with "A Tombstone Every Mile" and "Big Wheel Cannonball" being among the most memorable. (John Morris collection.)

Ramblin' Lou Schriver (1929–2016), a legendary deejay in the Buffalo, New York, area, started out solo. He eventually formed a family band and appeared several times yearly, always bringing busloads of *Jamboree* fans with him. A skilled performer himself, he tirelessly promoted country music in his region. Daughter Linda Lou became a *Jamboree* artist in her own right. (Williams family collection.)

Junior Norman (1933–1998) from Malta, Ohio, was a *Jamboree* regular during the 1970s. He also worked summers at Ponderosa Park, near Salem, Ohio, and recorded sparingly—three singles over his lifetime. Nonetheless, Norman had a broad repertoire and could sing all day long without repeating a song. (Williams family collection.)

Five

JAMBOREE BLUEGRASS
1948–2020

Bluegrass is a country music sub-type that came to full development in the mid-1940s. Although new, it harkened back to an earlier era that preceded electric instruments, jukeboxes, and loud dance halls. The principal creator was *Grand Ole Opry* artist Bill Monroe and various members of his Blue Grass Boys band, including Lester Flatt, Earl Scruggs, Chubby Wise, and Howard "Cedric Rainwater" Watts. High vocal harmonies, fiddle, mandolin, and finger-picked five-stringed banjo dominated the sound. Other bands predominantly located in Appalachian cities began to adopt what took the name "bluegrass" from Monroe's band and home state. Some elements of the music had been around earlier, but all of it came together at WWVA in 1952 and remained from then on with various groups at the *Jamboree*.

Earlier manifestations of bluegrass on the Virginia Theater stage came from the various duets that worked with clawhammer banjo picker Red Belcher, with such surnames as Hankinson, Ritchey, and especially Lilly in the 1947–1951 era. Wilma Lee and Stoney Cooper's music was almost bluegrass and later all bluegrass. Various bands of Toby Stroud also had a flavor that sometimes approached bluegrass. But it all came together with the Bailey Brothers and their Happy Valley Boys in the spring of 1952 and for the following two years. Later, other bluegrass bands came to Wheeling, such as Hylo Brown, Jim and Jesse (briefly), and most especially, the Osborne Brothers and Red Allen, who spent seven years (c. 1956–1964) at WWVA perfecting their vocal trio. From January 1960 until December 1962, Jimmy Martin and the Sunny Mountain Boys spent nearly three of their peak years in Wheeling. During the late 1960s, Mac Wiseman proved equally adept at either country or bluegrass, bringing such regulars to the stage as the bands of Jim Greer, Red Smiley, the Stanley Brothers, Charlie Moore and Bill Napier, and Jim Eanes. Cast members in the 1970s included the Shenandoah Cutups, Les Hall, Frank Necessary and the Stone Mountain Boys, and a returned Red Allen with his sons, the Allen Brothers.

The last decades of *Jamboree* history saw regional bands on the rolls, such as Mac Martin's Dixie Travelers, the Spirits of Bluegrass, the Short Crick Flatpickers, and the Wood Brothers. The current *Wheeling Jamboree* has the nationally known Larry Stephenson Band and Larry Efaw's Bluegrass Mountaineers. While never dominant, the bluegrass sound has usually been present.

A bluegrass legend, North Carolinian Arthur "Red" Smiley (1925–1972) earned most of his status as the partner of banjo picker Don Reno (1926–1984). They first appeared on the *Jamboree* in 1951. They were members of a band fronted by Toby Stroud. The two dissolved their partnership in 1964 with each one forming his own group. Red's Bluegrass Cutups did weekday morning television at Roanoke and worked the WWVA *Jamboree* on Saturday nights until 1969 when Smiley retired. He was one of the first bluegrass legends to pass away.

Toby Stroud (1921–1996) played music that varied between country and bluegrass. This band, the Blue Mountain Boys, came close to bluegrass with fiddler Buck Ryan (1925–1982) and mandolinist Bill Bailey (1921–?). Stroud recorded rousing versions of "Jesse James" and "Tragic Romance" in 1953. (Williams family collection.)

Jimmy Martin (1927–2005) became known as the "King of Bluegrass" with his quality vocals and hard-driving style. Like other bands, he and his Sunny Mountain Boys headquartered at several locales, notably the *Big Barn Frolic* in Detroit (1954–1958), *Louisiana Hayride* in Shreveport (1958–1959), *Jamboree* in Wheeling (1960–1962), and Nashville (1963–2005). This portrait dates from his WWVA years. (Williams family collection.)

When Kentucky-born, Springfield, Ohio, resident Frank "Hylo" Brown (1922–1995) landed a contract with Capitol Records in 1954, he formed a band, the Buckskin Boys, and landed a position at the *Jamboree*. Later, working solo, he led another band, the Timberliners, and recorded country and bluegrass for Starday, Rural Rhythm, and other labels. Many of his Rural Rhythm albums were produced by WWVA's Lee Sutton. Yet he never managed to equal his early successes. (Richard Weize and More Bears Archive.)

Ralph (1927–2016, on banjo) and Carter (1925–1966, on guitar), the Stanley Brothers, are usually considered one of the three most influential bluegrass acts of all time. However, their *Jamboree* membership was limited to the last year of Carter's failing health. Nonetheless, they remained on the road as long as Carter could bear it physically. (John Morris collection.)

The bluegrass brother team of Jim (1927–2002) and Jesse McReynolds (b. 1929) struggled to find their place in music for several years, including at the *Jamboree* in 1955. Eventually, they attained the deserved recognition, including *Opry* membership and the Bluegrass Hall of Honor (also known as the Hall of Fame).

Although Mac Wiseman had disbanded his band prior to coming to WWVA in 1965, his bluegrass recordings on Dot defined his legendary status. In this photograph, his band consisted of, from left to right, Lee Coles, Buck Graves, Don Bryant, and Curtis Lee. Wiseman is seated in front. Graves had an earlier career at WWVA, with Wilma Lee and Stoney Cooper and a later one with Lester Flatt and Earl Scruggs.

Benjamin "Tex" Logan (1929–2015) played fiddle at WWVA with Red Belcher's Cumberland Ridge Runners before moving on to New England, where he obtained a PhD from Massachusetts Institute of Technology (MIT), playing in Boston with the Lane Brothers and with Jerry and Sky. He enticed the Lilly Brothers to come to Boston, where they became musical legends. Here, Logan is flanked by Everett Lilly (left) and Bea Lilly (right). (Terrence McGill collection.)

Danny and Charlie, the Bailey Brothers, exhibited the same level of quality professionalism at WWVA that they had displayed at earlier locations in Raleigh, Knoxville, and Nashville. Their fiddler Tater Tate reminisced in 1973 that of all the bands he worked with, none could draw crowds or please audiences better than the Baileys. Sadly, they recorded sparingly in their early years but did a couple of albums for Rounder during the 1970s. (Williams family collection.)

From 1965 until 1969, Arthur "Red" Smiley (1925–1972) and the Bluegrass Cutups worked weekday mornings at WDBJ Roanoke and most Saturday nights at the *Jamboree*. Making up this lineup are, from left to right, Billy Edwards (banjo), Clarence "Tater" Tate (fiddle) Red Smiley (guitar), John Palmer (bass), and Gene Burroughs (guitar). Organist Irving Sharp, at bottom, only worked with them at Roanoke. Lee Sutton of WWVA produced their Rural Rhythm record albums.

Sometime during their 1956–1958 days at the *Jamboree*, from left to right, Red Allen, Bobby Osborne, and Sonny Osborne relax for a moment. Allen departed in 1958 to be succeeded by Ray Anderson, Jimmy Brown, and others in the trio. The Osbornes left WWVA for the *Grand Ole Opry* in 1964, where Bobby continues performing; Sonny retired some years ago. (Richard Weize and More Bears Archive.)

Bob Osborne (b. 1931), Sonny Osborne (b. 1937), and Red Allen (1930–1993) perfected their bluegrass trio during their *Jamboree* years (1956–1964) with songs like "Once More" and "Ruby." After Allen departed, others, such as Jimmy Brown and Ray Anderson, did his part. The brothers eventually moved on to the *Opry*, but only Bob remains active in 2020. (Terrence McGill collection.)

Frank Necessary (1935–2011) and the Stone Mountain Boys were a popular *Jamboree* bluegrass band in the late 1960s and early 1970s recording for Cabut and Old Homestead. This version consisted of Larry Fowler (guitar), Frank Necessary (banjo), Les Fiber (bass), and Robert "Buck" McCumbers (mandolin). Necessary later played around Washington and Baltimore, while McCumbers and his brother Dwayne are part of Buck & Co. in the Parkersburg area. (Buck McCumbers collection.)

For several years from 1969, the Shenandoah Cutups were *Jamboree* favorites. Pictured here are Billy Edwards, Wesley Golding, John Palmer, Clarence "Tater" Tate, and Herschel Sizemore. (Williams family collection.)

Larry Efaw and the Bluegrass Mountaineers have been the leading bluegrass band in the Akron area for several years and also *Jamboree* regulars. This photograph, which may precede their *Jamboree* affiliation, shows Efaw in the second row, far right. The others are not identified.

Banjo and mandolin picker Jim Greer led a bluegrass band from his West Liberty, Ohio, home, spending the late 1960s with the *Jamboree* and proving popular at county fairs throughout the Midwest and Pennsylvania. The Mac-O-Chee Valley Folks consisted of John Wentz (dobro), Bob McPherson (mandolin), Valeda Greer Wentz (guitar), Dalton Burroughs (bass), and Jim Greer (banjo).

JIM GREER and the MAC-O-CHEE VALLEY FOLKS

The Short Crick Flatpickers, a Wheeling-area band that helped revive interest in bluegrass in the local area, worked at the *Jamboree* for several years in the 1980s. They also often played at Ogleby Park and recorded two albums on Old Homestead Records. From left to right are Jeff Strectman (bass), Tom White (guitar), John Angius (mandolin), and Ed Mahonien (banjo).

Charlie Moore (1935–1979) had one of the clearest voices in bluegrass. His initial *Jamboree* sojourn took place from 1964 to 1967, with his first partner Bill Napier. In the 1970s, he returned with his Dixie Partners and recorded several albums for Old Homestead and Vetco. He died at 44 from a liver ailment. (John Morris collection.)

Six

FADING IN THE SUNSET—ALMOST
1983–2020

The golden anniversary marked the zenith for the later years of *Jamboree USA*. The pattern established in the late 1970s continued for another decade or so with little change. Guest stars continued to dominate the lineup, with a few regulars as opening acts and more cast members in the latter part of December. A highlight came on May 19, 1987, when Doc Williams celebrated his 50 years at WWVA with family members and close associates like Roy Scott joining in the festivities. Eddy Arnold played a special matinee show in 1993, but from then on, the trend drifted downward. AM radio declined in influence only to be somewhat rescued by the rise of talk radio, whether syndicated, local, or sports, a format pushed by Clear Channel, a new media giant that had no real place for programs like *Jamboree USA*. Crowds declined, and on many Saturdays, no shows were scheduled. At the end of 2005, the respected live program ended its long run, although rerun tapes of old shows continued for a time

Ironically, while the *Jamboree* proper was going the route of the Roman Empire, Jamboree in the Hills continued to grow and prosper. In 1990, it outgrew the Alderman-owned Brush Run Park and moved to larger acreage. Major stars dominated. In 2017, fans could see Lee Greenwood, Lady Antebellum, Aaron Tippen, and Tanya Tucker. The next year's attractions included Charlie Daniels, Travis Tritt, Gretchen Wilson, and Joe Diffie, among others. No Jamboree in the Hills was held in 2019, and at this writing, its future remains in doubt.

Meanwhile, a small group of *Jamboree* loyalists made efforts to continue the program on smaller stations and in modest venues around the city. In January 2008, a newly organized nonprofit, Wheeling Jamboree, Inc., completed the transition from WWVA radio "to the Nonprofit Organization." A local man, David Heath, emerged as executive director. Results thus far have been mixed and mostly modest. Some regulars from the past, such as the late Leon Douglas and Darnell Miller, made periodic returns. Some bigger names have appeared; Charlie McCoy, Ronnie Millsap, and Bill Anderson and younger female vocalist Shana Smith have proved to be crowd-pleasers. However, many of the crowds have been small, and keeping the program and station WWOV alive has been a struggle.

Connie Smith (b. 1941) grew up within the WWVA listening area in Warner, Ohio. She went from appearing on local television to top stardom in the mid-1960s. Eventually curtailing extensive travel, she kept appearing on the *Grand Ole Opry* but was always a popular guest on the *Jamboree* from 1966 and at Jamboree in the Hills. She remained a loyal fan of Doc and Chickie Williams. (Williams family collection.)

Charlie Daniels (1938–2020) developed a musical style that combined elements of rock, country, and bluegrass into a sound that led him to the Country Music Hall of Fame. He proved popular as a name guest both at the *Jamboree* and Jamboree in the Hills. He was also a Doc Williams fan. (Williams family collection.)

Leon Douglas (1939–2017), whom one fan described as the *Jamboree*'s most solid regular performer in the program's last three decades, returned to the post-WWVA in early 2014 for a final appearance, where it is obvious that the years were beginning to take their toll. A classic honky-tonk vocalist, Douglas could shine on songs like "The Friday Night Fights." (Dave Heath collection.)

A *Jamboree* favorite of the program's last three decades, Leon Douglas posed with country superstar Loretta Lynn, the celebrated "Coal Miner's Daughter" who became a symbol of the American Dream with her rags-to-riches story. Lynn was one of many popular guest stars of the system launched by Mac Wiseman in 1966 and thereafter. (Dave Heath collection.)

One of the three daughters of WWVA legend Ramblin' Roy Scott, Lois Scott (b. 1956) led a rock-flavored country band, Back Up and Push, at the *Jamboree* beginning in 1986. Sisters Janice and Lori also sometimes worked with her in music. At the time of her father's death in 2010, Lois resided in White Oak, Pennsylvania, with her husband, Mark Novakovich. (Williams family collection.)

Bill Ross Jr. and Crazy Roy (Hanna Jr.) were *Jamboree* regulars in the program's later years. They recorded on the Gallery II label. Other than that, little information on them has surfaced. (Williams family collection.)

Mayf Nutter (b. 1941) came from a musical family in the town of Jane Lew, West Virginia. He made his first radio appearance at WPDX with Cherokee Sue. In addition to the *Jamboree*, he worked on Buck Owens's television show and had seven songs on the charts.

Slim Lehart

"The Wheeling Cat" Slim Lehart stayed active in the Wheeling area after his WWVA career. He was active in local politics. Until recently, he was a regular at a local eatery for breakfast, where he would regale other diners with a variety of songs and stories. Sadly, as of this writing, he is suffering severe health issues.

With their careers winding down, Doc and Chickie Williams performed less and less and often just with their daughters and another musician or two. This photograph from 1996, originally in color, shows, from left to right, Madeline ("Poochie"), Karen ("Punkin"), Chickie, and Barbara ("Pepper"), with Doc seated in front with a guitar. Doc last appeared on the *Jamboree* in 2004.

Roger Hoard was a member of the *Jamboree* band for more than 30 years, sometimes as a leader and nearly always on lead guitar, winning praise from musicians such as Buddy Griffin, vocalists like Karen McKenzie, and pupils such as Brad Paisley.

Roger Hoard (right) jams with his most famous pupil, Brad Paisley. (Roger Hoard collection.)

Brad Paisley (b. 1972) was a familiar figure at the *Jamboree* from the age of 14, usually as a member of the staff band and soloist, learning guitar from Roger Hoard and the business from legend Doc Williams, for whom he signed this photograph in 1992. He later moved to Nashville and, within a few years, attained superstar status. (Williams family collection.)

Mac Martin (b. 1925 as William Colleran) and the Dixie Travelers were a traditional bluegrass legend in Pittsburgh and beyond for nearly six decades. From the late 1980s, they were regulars on the *Jamboree* cast. A widely acclaimed vintage bluegrass band, they have recorded many albums. This band lineup from the late 1980s shows, from left to right, Buzz Matheson, Mike Carson, Norm Azinger, Mac Martin, and Billy Bryant.

Shana Smith is one of the featured performers at the contemporary *Wheeling Jamboree* no longer affiliated with WWVA but heard over WWOV-FM. Smith, a resident of Gallia County, Ohio, has two compact discs to her credit, one of largely originals and another of standards recorded live at the *Jamboree* in 2013. She also cowrote a children's book about a grasshopper, *Sheldon and the Big Hurricane* (2015).

One of the best public school bluegrass programs is that of Wheeling Park High School. Over the years, they have appeared several times on the *Jamboree*. However, the personnel changes every year. (Robert Turbanic collection.)

Members of the 2004 Wheeling Park bluegrass group pose at the *Jamboree* with Tim and Mollie O'Brien. (Robert Turbanic collection.)

Pictured are, from left to right, Darnell Miller, Dave Heath (Wheeling *Jamboree* CEO), Shana

Smith, and Keith Bilbrey (Wheeling *Jamboree* board member). (David Smith photograph.)

Betty Lou Miller (b. 1942), better known as Margo Smith, became a kindergarten teacher who sang on the side. She became a regular on the *Jamboree* about 1974 and eventually gained major label contracts and relocated to Nashville. Over a 13-year period, she had 27 chart makers, including two number ones; most were on the Warner Bros. label.

Tom, Bill, and Harry Compton hailed from Missouri and signed with Columbia in 1965. They moved to the Dot label in 1966, making the Billboard charts 13 times through 1975. They joined the *Jamboree* in 1968, although Tom soon departed. Their best remembered songs were country versions of rock and roll hits from a decade and earlier such as "Haunted House," "Charlie Brown," and "Claudette" as well as Jimmie Rodgers's "California Blues." (Williams family collection.)

Built in the late 1920s, the Capitol Theater in downtown Wheeling served as the *Jamboree* home from 1933 to 1934 and again from late 1969 until December 2005. Depending on seating changes, it could hold anywhere from over 2,400 persons to more than 3,000. For special shows, the *Jamboree* was held there at other times. This photograph by Deanna Tribe was made in 1981.

Betty Amos with Judy and Jean
Starday Records - WWVA Jamboree

Judy Lee Agency
P.O. Box 128- Hendersonville, Tenn.
Code 615 824-8552 37075

Banjo-picking Betty Amos (b. 1934, right) grew up near Roanoke, Virginia, and began her career with the Carlisles. She went solo after a year. In 1960, she teamed up with her younger sister Jean (center) and Judy Lee (left). Dividing their base between WWVA and KWKH, they worked together until 1977 when they retired from music. In 2013, all three lived in Hendersonville, Tennessee. (Williams family collection.)

Shana Smith is seen on stage at the 84th anniversary of the *Jamboree*. (Suzanne McVay

Polinski photograph.)

When Mac Wiseman introduced the guest star system in 1966, Opry star Bill Anderson (b. 1937)—then at the peak of his career—was his first. Anderson guested on the *Jamboree* several times over the next five decades. He is pictured here with one of his most loyal fans, Janet Bapst. (Janet Bapst photograph.)

Ivan Tribe is professor emeritus of history at the University of Rio Grande in Ohio. Through his writing of 14 books to numerous magazine articles to a weekly radio show he hosts with his wife, Deanna, he has worked to keep traditional and bluegrass music alive. He is pictured with legends and friends Doc Williams (left) and Grandpa Jones (right). Deanna said one day at breakfast that Ivan remarked, "You know, I have met some interesting people at the *Jamboree*." (Barbara Smik photograph.)

Discover Thousands of Local History Books Featuring Millions of Vintage Images

Arcadia Publishing, the leading local history publisher in the United States, is committed to making history accessible and meaningful through publishing books that celebrate and preserve the heritage of America's people and places.

Find more books like this at
www.arcadiapublishing.com

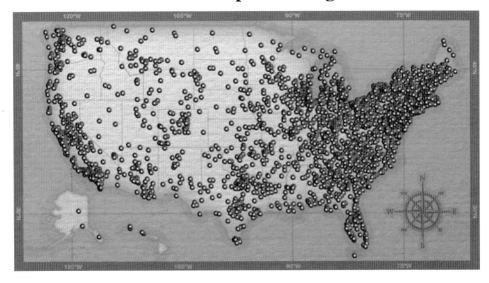

Search for your hometown history, your old stomping grounds, and even your favorite sports team.

Consistent with our mission to preserve history on a local level, this book was printed in South Carolina on American-made paper and manufactured entirely in the United States. Products carrying the accredited Forest Stewardship Council (FSC) label are printed on 100 percent FSC-certified paper.